# SEASONAL
## SCANDI CRAFTS

# SEASONAL
# SCANDI CRAFTS

**over 45** projects and
quick ideas for beautiful
decorations & gifts

## CHRISTIANE BELLSTEDT MYERS

Photography by Caroline Arber

**CICO BOOKS**
LONDON  NEW YORK

**To my family and kindred spirits who make my house a home x**

Published in 2019 by CICO Books
An imprint of Ryland Peters & Small Ltd
20–21 Jockey's Fields, London WC1R 4BW
341 E 116th St, New York, NY 10029

www.rylandpeters.com

10 9 8 7 6 5 4 3 2 1

Text © Christiane Bellstedt Myers 2019
Design, illustration, and photography
© CICO Books 2019

A CIP catalog record for this book is available from the Library of Congress and the British Library.

ISBN: 978-1-78249-689-2

Printed in China

Editor: Clare Sayer
Designer: Alison Fenton
Photographer: Caroline Arber
Illustrator: Stephen Dew
Stylists: Sophie Martell and Kerry Lewis

In-house editor: Anna Galkina
Art director: Sally Powell
Production controller: David Hearn
Publishing manager: Penny Craig
Publisher: Cindy Richards

# contents

# introduction

I have always loved the seasons. They are steeped in traditions and unwritten laws of bygone days. They are welcomed with excitement and anticipation, each bringing a constant reminder that life goes on. It is the idea of renewal and hope that enthralls all of us. Every season brings with it a bounty of produce and flora; nothing is more magical when wandering along a lane on a late winter's day than suddenly coming across a glorious clump of snowdrops about to burst open. My thoughts turn immediately to spring and I cannot wait to get home and start creating a fresh look to reflect this time. This can be said for each season and year after year the excitement never wanes—that is what I cherish.

In Scandinavia seasons play a very important role in day-to-day life. The harsh winters require planning and foresight. There is great importance placed upon respecting the changes of temperature, and celebrations for each time of year create much joy. From the gorgeous candlelit traditions at Christmas time to celebrating the summer solstice, Scandinavians relish their yearly convivial rituals.

This book is laid out in four distinct chapters to embrace each time of year. All projects are inspired by the Nordic way of life of simplicity and usefulness. Effort has been made to reuse materials, whether wood, fabric, or metal. For example, many of the nails used in these projects were in fact embedded in old wood—whenever I have a bonfire I rake through the cold ashes to collect any nails or scraps of metal. When doing this I like to wonder about the person who used all my repurposed items before and what their lives were like.

Our changing seasons give us a regular opportunity to renew, redecorate, and rejoice. I do hope that you will gather some ideas from the projects outlined in this book and be able to welcome each sweet time of year with much delight and exult in each one as I do.

With love from my seasonal home to yours.

Chris xx

# CHAPTER 1

## spring

SPRING. THE NAME ALONE MAKES YOU WANT TO SKIP FOR JOY. THOSE FIRST FEW DAYS WHEN THE SUN BEGINS TO WARM THE AIR ARE NOTHING SHORT OF MIRACULOUS. EVERY YEAR WE ALL EXCLAIM OVER THE BEAUTY THAT NATURE PRESENTS TO US, WITH ITS PROMISE OF NEW BEGINNINGS. THE DAWN CHORUS MAKES EARLY MORNINGS ALL THE MORE ENJOYABLE, WHILE THE DIFFERENT HUES OF GREEN AROUND US, FROM ACID GREEN TO STUNNING EMERALD AND EVERYTHING IN BETWEEN, ARE SIMPLY AMAZING. FRESH BLADES OF GRASS THAT GLIMMER IN A DEW-FILLED MORNING; SUNLIGHT GLISTENING OFF RAINDROPS; BLOSSOMS THAT APPEAR AS IF BY MAGIC. ONE MINUTE THERE IS A SHIMMER OF COLOR ON A TREE THEN ALL OF A SUDDEN IT BURSTS FORTH WITH DELICATE PETALS IN WHITE OR PINK. SPRING IGNITES THE DESIRE TO RENEW OUR HOME, CLEAR AWAY THE HEAVY COLORS OF WINTER, LET IN THE LIGHT, OPEN THE WINDOWS, AND BREATHE IN THE FRESH AIR. THESE SPRINGTIME PROJECTS WILL HOPEFULLY BURST OPEN YOUR CREATIVITY. SO PREPARE YOUR WORKSPACE, MAKE SOME TEA, AND THEN HAVE SOME FUN. WELCOME SPRING!

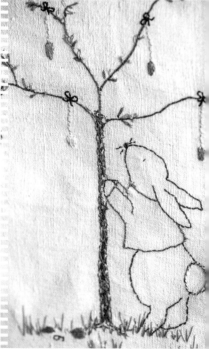

# spring indoor window box

WHEN SPRING ARRIVES NOTHING FEELS BETTER THAN TO GO OUT AND PICK SOME OF THE VERY FIRST BLOOMS OF THE SEASON. HAVING A CLUSTER OF CANS MEANS IT IS EASY TO GET THE FEELING OF ABUNDANCE WITHOUT HAVING TO BUY OR PICK TOO MANY FLOWERS. WHY NOT FILL THEM WITH POTS OF FRESH HERBS AS WELL? THEY WILL LOOK GREAT AND DELIVER BOTH SCENT AND USEFULNESS IN THE KITCHEN.

## MATERIALS

Old rectangular wooden box

Cream paint (I used water-based eggshell)

Empty cans

Scraps of linen fabric

Embroidery floss (thread)

Buttons (optional)

Old newspaper or printed paper

Fresh flowers, spring bulbs, or fresh herbs in pots

## TOOLS

Paintbrush

Needle

Pencil

Scissors

Spring motif templates (see page 123)

Cookie cutters (optional)

White craft (PV) glue

**1** Make sure the surface of your box is clean and dry and then paint it, inside and out, with cream paint. You may need to add a second coat so allow to dry between coats. Do the same with the empty cans.

**2** Cut a few small rectangles from the linen fabric. Using a needle and stranded embroidery floss (thread), stitch a motif onto each one, using the stitch techniques on pages 107–112. Choose spring motifs such as flowers, chicks, or little wreaths (see page 123). You only need a few to give the box its own unique character. Add a few small buttons here and there if you have some to hand.

**3** Use a pencil to draw various shapes onto the newspaper, such as ducks, hearts, and rabbits. If you have some shaped cookie cutters to hand, use those, or use the templates on 123.

**4** Glue the various embellishments onto the box, not forgetting the ends. The cans get a touch of decoration as well. Finally, fill the cans with fresh flowers or herbs. This window box looks equally delightful on a mantle or shelf and shouts "spring is here."

Long ago, most elegant dinners required large, starched white napkins and these would often be monogrammed. These gorgeous memories of past times have been relegated to the back corners of cupboards, forgotten and unused. Because of their large size they can have multiple uses—I have found them to be the perfect size to make curtains for my little windows. The most wonderful bonus in using napkins is that they are already hemmed so very little stitching is required. It is always fun to try and find a monogram that matches your name; the one shown here is that of my mother.

## MATERIALS

Antique linen napkins

Net curtain wire

Hooks and eyes

## TOOLS

Scissors

Needle and sewing thread

Wire cutters or pliers

**1** Depending on the size of your window you may need to sew a few napkin squares together—the width of the curtain needs to be at least twice that of the window to make a charming gathered curtain. Simply stitch together with a ½ in. (1 cm) seam allowance and then press the seams flat.

**2** Fold the top of the napkin curtain over to the wrong side, just enough to make a channel for the curtain wire to fit through, and stitch.

**3** Cut the net curtain wire to the correct length with wire cutters or pliers and then thread through the channel in the napkin curtain. Gather the curtain evenly along the wire. Attach the hooks and eyes and simply attach the curtain wire to each side of the window.

# quick idea BUTTON BLOSSOM JAR

Collections of old buttons can be found at any flea market or thrift store. There was a time when nothing was ever thrown away; the thinking being that in time they may be needed once again. I can never pass by an old tin or jar of buttons. Dreams of old farmhouses with children rushing through the door holding another lost button to add to the jar fills my imagination. One day, while admiring my button collection I wondered how I could use them so that I could see them daily. This is what I came up with: flowers, buttons, and an old jar to create a thing of beauty to me.

## MATERIALS

Buttons

Old jars

Flowers

**1** Pour a handful of buttons into an old jar—you only need to fill the bottom couple of inches.

**2** Add clean water and a few blossoms and that's it! These are lovely displayed in small groups; it didn't take me long to fill a few of these, which leaves me ready to go on another button hunt!

# lavender pillow
THE THOUGHT OF REUSING A MUCH LOVED AND WORN QUILT TO MAKE SOMETHING DELICATE AND CHARMING IN THIS THROWAWAY WORLD IS VERY PLEASING TO ME. HAVING KEPT GENERATIONS WARM AND SNUG, THIS RED AND WHITE QUILT WILL NOW GO ON TO SCENT A ROOM AND DELIGHT THE EYE WITH THE SMALL STITCHERIES THAT EMBELLISH IT. IT IS ALSO LOVELY TO GIVE AS A PRESENT—I MADE ONE FOR MY MOTHER FOR HER 85TH BIRTHDAY AND INCLUDED LITTLE POCKETS WHERE I WROTE TINY NOTES FOR HER TO FIND. THE OLD QUILT IS JUST THE STARTING POINT. WHAT YOU ADD IS UP TO YOU AND YOUR IMAGINATION.

## MATERIALS

Piece of old quilt

Backing fabric

Embroidery floss (thread)

Fabric scraps

Buttons

Toy stuffing

Dried lavender

## TOOLS

Scissors

Pins

Needle and matching sewing thread

**1** Decide what size you would like your lavender pillow to be. Cut a piece from the old quilt to this size, adding ½ in. (1 cm) all round to allow for the seams. Cut the backing fabric to the same size. Using two strands of embroidery floss (thread), add small stitchery designs such as hearts and flowers onto the quilt (see pages 107–112). I like to add a few fabric scraps and buttons to give interest.

**2** When you are happy with the look of your little pillow pin the backing fabric to the quilt piece right sides together. Stitch the pieces together with a ½ in. (1 cm) seam allowance, leaving a gap at one short end for the stuffing and lavender.

**3** Turn the pillow right side out. I added some stuffing to this pillow to give it more shape, particularly in the corners, but that is up to you. Add the dried lavender and more stuffing if you wish.

**4** Turn the edges under at the opening and slipstitch the opening closed. Give it a good shake to distribute the lavender. I love to leave these dotted around the house on stools and beds. I believe that the quilter who made this quilt would only be too happy to see it being loved once more.

# may day hanging tin

WHO WOULD NOT BE UTTERLY OVERWHELMED WHEN OPENING THEIR DOOR TO FIND A BEAUTIFUL POSY OF BLOOMS HANGING FROM THE DOORKNOB? LONG AGO, THE CUSTOM WAS TO DELIVER THESE LITTLE SURPRISES TO FRIENDS AND FAMILY ON THE FIRST DAY OF MAY. I THINK IT IS A LOVELY TRADITION BUT IT CAN BE USED FOR OTHER SPECIAL DAYS AS WELL, SUCH AS MOTHER'S DAY, BIRTHDAYS, OR ANNIVERSARIES. IMAGINING THE DELIGHT AND SURPRISE ON THE RECIPIENT'S FACE IS ALMOST THE BEST PART.

**1** Make sure your can is clean and dry and then paint it inside and out. Leave to dry completely.

**2** Measure the circumference of the can and then cut enough lace fabric to wrap around it, covering the entire can.

**3** Sew the two ends of the lace fabric together so that the tin slips into the fabric (you want it to fit quite tightly).

**4** Cut a length of fabric and shape it into a loop; sew this to the top of the fabric sleeve where the seam is. Pull the sleeve over the can, fill with water, add your blossoms and then go and delight someone!

## MATERIALS

Clean can

Cream paint (I use water-based eggshell)

Piece of old lace fabric (I find plenty at all the wonderful vintage fairs throughout the year)

Fresh blossoms

## TOOLS

Paintbrush

Tape measure

Scissors

Needle and matching sewing thread

# old bottle vase

HAVING FRESH FLOWERS IN YOUR HOME IS ALWAYS A JOY. SOMETIMES, HOWEVER, ONE OR TWO BLOOMS ARE AS BEAUTIFUL AS A HUGE BOUQUET. USING SMALL BOTTLES MAKES THE PERFECT VESSEL TO ENJOY THEM AND ATTACHING THESE BOTTLES TO A DECORATIVE PIECE OF WOOD TO BE HUNG ON A WALL ELEVATES THE BOTTLE AND BLOOM TO A WORK OF ART. TAKE YOUR TIME WHEN CUTTING OUT THE HEART TO GIVE YOURSELF A PLEASING SHAPE. WHEN SOURCING YOUR PIECE OF WOOD IT IS LOVELY IF YOU CAN FIND AN OLD PIECE WITH A DISTRESSED OR AGED PAINT FINISH.

## MATERIALS

Piece of old wood

Screws

Wire

Small strip of wood

Nails

Small glass bottle

## TOOLS

Heart-shaped cookie cutter (or use the heart template on page 123)

Pencil

Small jigsaw

Sandpaper

Wire cutters

Hammer

Hand drill

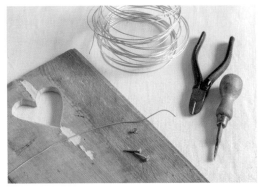

**1** Using either a cookie cutter or the template on page 123, draw a heart shape onto the wood. Carefully cut out the shape, using a small jigsaw. Use a small piece of sandpaper to smooth down the cut edges.

**2** Turn the piece of wood over and attach two screws either side of the wood, just below the heart. Cut a length of wire and twist it around the screws to create a wire to hang the wood to the wall.

**3** Now attach a small strip of wood to the bottom edge of the back of the piece of wood, using a hammer and small nails. This will ensure that the bottle hangs straight.

**hint** Add a small nail to the front of the wood just below the bottom of the bottle to support it, especially if your bottle is a heavy one.

**4** Turn the wood over. As all old bottles are different, measure your bottle and decide where you want to attach the wire to hold the bottle. You need to mark four holes to hold two different wires. Use a hand drill to make the holes, then attach the bottle by threading two lengths of wire through the holes and twisting them at the back to secure it. Before filling the bottle with water, make sure the bottle is on straight and tight. Add your favorite blossoms, stand back, and enjoy the view.

# easter stitchery

I HAVE BEEN CREATING STITCHERIES FOR FRIENDS AND FAMILY AS PRESENTS FOR MANY YEARS. AT THE COZY CLUB MANY PROJECTS HAVE INCLUDED ELEMENTS OF EMBROIDERY AND SOMETIMES, WHEN A PROJECT THAT LOOKS DIFFICULT IS INTRODUCED, A DISBELIEVING LOOK CROSSES OVER SOME FACES. CAROLINE ZOOB, A WISE AND TALENTED MENTOR, ONCE SAID EMBROIDERY IS "JUST PAINTING WITH A NEEDLE". MISTAKES WILL BE MADE BUT ALL ARE EASILY RECTIFIED. THIS STITCHERY HAS ONLY A FEW SIMPLE STITCHES BUT THROUGH COLOR AND TEXTURE A SWEET AND ENCHANTING PICTURE IS CREATED. EXPERIMENT AND HAVE FUN!

## MATERIALS

Linen fabric, 10 x 12 in. (26 x 31 cm)

Embroidery floss (thread) in assorted colors

Picture frame

Narrow ribbon

## TOOLS

Template on page 117

Friction pen

Fabric scissors

Embroidery scissors

Embroidery needle

Iron

Staple gun

Fabric glue

Paintbrush

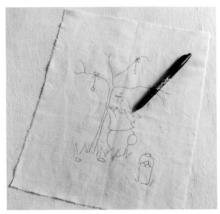

**1** Using the template on page 117 and a friction pen, transfer the design onto your piece of linen fabric.

**2** Using your chosen colors of embroidery floss (thread) stitch over your outline (see pages 107–112 for the various stitch techniques). I use just one or two strands of floss at a time as it makes the picture look much more delicate and you can always go over an area if you want it more pronounced.

**3** Once you are happy with your stitchery, iron it gently on the wrong side and trim away any loose threads. Then attach onto the backing board of your frame using a staple gun, making sure everything is straight and neat.

**4** Place it carefully into the frame and secure it. As a final unique touch I decorated the edge of the stitchery by adding a rim of narrow ribbon. Using a dark colored ribbon really makes the stitchery pop out and also makes it extra special. Glue the ribbon around the inside edge of the frame.

# gardening apron

GATHERING THE TOOLS NECESSARY TO COMPLETE SIMPLE GARDENING JOBS IS ALWAYS THE FIRST TICK ON MY LIST. AS ANY GARDENER KNOWS, HAVING MORE THAN TWO HANDS IS CERTAINLY WELCOME BUT NOT ALWAYS AVAILABLE! THIS PROMPTED ME TO CREATE AN APRON ESPECIALLY FOR THE GARDEN—THERE ARE POCKETS TO HOLD SECATEURS AND PLANT LABELS BUT THE IMPORTANT FEATURE IS A POCKET WITH A SMALL HOLE IN IT; THIS POCKET HOLDS A BALL OF STRING AND THE END OF THE STRING CAN BE PULLED OUT THROUGH THE HOLE TO ANY LENGTH DESIRED.

## MATERIALS

Length of strong fabric, approximately 30 x 17 in. (76 x 43 cm), ideally with no right or wrong side

80 in. (204 cm) strong woven ribbon for the apron ties

Small piece of red gingham fabric, 8 x 2 in. (20 x 5 cm)

## TOOLS

Scissors

Needle and matching sewing thread

Embroidery scissors

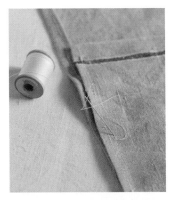

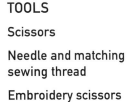

**1** Start by folding and stitching a small double hem, about ½ in. (1 cm), along each side of the fabric. Fold the bottom half of the fabric up to create a pocket that is 9 in. (23 cm) deep. Sew down both sides of the pocket leaving the long edge open at the top. Sew a seam down the pocket to create another pocket to hold items such as secateurs or plant labels; I sewed one 5 in. (13 cm) from the opposite edge.

**2** Using small sharp scissors such as embroidery scissors, cut a small hole in the larger of the pockets. This is for the twine or string. Make sure it is not too big. Sew around the edge of the hole using a buttonhole stitch (see page 111).

**3** Cut the strong woven ribbon to create two lengths, each 49 in. (102 cm) long. Attach each length of ribbon to either side of the top of the apron.

**4** Take the gingham fabric and fold and press both short edges in by ¼ in. (5 mm). Now fold each long edge in toward the center and then fold in half lengthwise to hide the raw edges. Stitch closed, close to the fold. You will have a piece of finished fabric resembling a thick ribbon. Fold this in half and attach to the outside of the apron. This is ideal to hold a hand towel or, as seen on page 37, the mending kit.

# rabbit pillow

AFTER A LONG WINTER WE ALL LOOK FORWARD TO THE FIRST SHOOTS OF NATURE'S GREENERY WITH HUGE ANTICIPATION. WELCOMING IN THE SPRING SEASON BY ADDING A LOVELY PILLOW OR TWO IS A CHARMING WAY TO USHER IN THIS NEW TIME OF YEAR. ALL YOU NEED TO INCLUDE ARE SOME SWEET BLOOMING FLOWERS AND YOU WILL BE WELL ON YOUR WAY. FOR THE PATCHWORK FABRIC I USED A BEAUTIFUL QUILT TOP GIVEN TO ME BY MY MOTHER'S DEAR FRIEND FROM MY HOMETOWN OF KINCARDINE, CANADA.

## MATERIALS

Fusible bonding web

Piece of wool blanket

Patterned fabric scraps (for the egg and heart)

Linen fabric square, 17 x 17 in. (42 x 42 cm)

Green gingham fabric square, 8 x 8 in. (20 x 20 cm)

Button

Embroidery floss (thread)

Patchwork fabric

16 in. (40 cm) pillow pad

## TOOLS

Iron

Templates on page 118

Rabbit cookie cutter (optional)

Friction pen

Scissors

Tape measure

Needle and matching sewing thread

Sewing machine (optional)

Pins

**1** Following the manufacturer's instructions, iron the fusible bonding web to the wrong side of the piece of wool blanket, as well as to the fabrics you have chosen for the egg and heart.

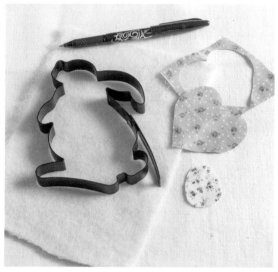

**2** Use the templates on page 118 and a friction pen to draw a rabbit shape onto the right side of the blanket piece (or use a rabbit cookie cutter) and the heart and egg shapes onto the patterned scraps. Cut out the three shapes.

**3** Peel the backing paper away from the back of the heart and position in the center of the linen square. Following the instructions, use a hot iron to fuse the fabrics together. Do the same with the rabbit and egg, positioning them on the right side of the gingham square.

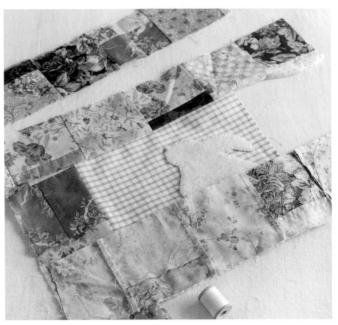

**4** Sew a small decorative button to the top of the heart. Using two strands of pale cream embroidery floss (thread), blanket stitch around the rabbit, egg, and heart (see page 108). Stitch a small nose onto the rabbit, using a contrasting color.

**5** Cut out and assemble your pieces of fabric for the front of the pillow. You will need to cut four strips of fabric measuring 17 x 5 in. (42 x 12 cm). Using a sewing machine or needle and thread, stitch these to the center panel to make a wide border. The finished front piece should be 17 in. (42 cm) square. Press all the seams open.

**6** Place the front and back pieces right sides together and pin together. Sew all around the edges with a ½ in. (1 cm) seam allowance, leaving a gap in one edge to insert the pillow pad. Trim the seam allowances and press the seams open, then turn the cover the right way out. Insert the pillow pad and then slipstitch the opening closed (see page 107).

# quick idea BOX OF HEARTS

Hearts could almost be the national symbol of the countries of Scandinavia as they are used throughout the year, in all sorts of ways. The shape exudes warmth and love, both of which are true characteristics of these lands. I have collected hearts for many years, trying to find unique ones from the past. I found this box complete with wallpaper dating from the 1800s and immediately realized it could only be filled with something beautiful and soft. My growing collection of hand-made lavender hearts sits happily in this box and from time to time a new heart made from old fabric will be added.

## MATERIALS

Scraps of red and white fabric

Dried lavender

## TOOLS

Templates on page 122

Scissors

Needle and matching sewing thread

**1** Using the templates on page 122, cut from your fabric two heart shapes for every one heart you wish to make.

**2** With right sides together, stitch the heart pieces together, leaving a gap in one side.

**3** Turn the heart right side out and fill with dried lavender. Slipstitch the gap closed. I know one will not be enough so be sure to cut quite a few hearts!

# valentine's heart wreath

HEARTS ARE EVERYWHERE IN SCANDINAVIA. I STARTED COLLECTING THEM YEARS AGO BUT HAVE NARROWED DOWN MY COLLECTION TO INCLUDE MAINLY VINTAGE HEARTS, PARTICULARLY COOKIE CUTTERS. EVERYWHERE I GO I SEARCH FOR THESE SIMPLE SHAPES; WHEN I DISCOVER ONE IT FEELS LIKE FINDING MY POT OF GOLD. I KEEP THEM IN OLD MASON JARS AND WILL OFTEN TIE ONE ONTO A PRESENT FOR SOMEONE SPECIAL. THIS WREATH ALLOWS ME TO ENJOY THESE WONDERFUL SHAPES ALL AT ONCE—WITH JUST A PINCH OF GLITTER THE HUMBLE HEART SHAPE BECOMES A BEAUTIFUL DECORATIVE ITEM TO CHEER UP A PLAIN WHITE WALL.

## MATERIALS

Circle of wire (look in hobby stores or make one out of strong wire)

Selection of old or new tin hearts—cookie cutters, cake tins, and jelly molds all work well

Glass glitter (optional)

Ribbon

Greenery

## TOOLS

Hot glue gun

White craft (PVA) glue

**1** Lay your circle of wire on the table and decide where your hearts should go. Using the hot glue gun, carefully glue the shapes onto the wire. It is very easy to remove the glue and reposition the hearts should you need to.

**2** Add a sprinkling of glass glitter to the darker heart shapes if you like. A little dab of white craft (PVA) glue will help it stick nicely.

**3** Tie a pretty ribbon to the top of the wreath—I find that a simple narrow ribbon works best.

**4** Add some fresh greenery to celebrate the season. Here I have used snowberries but you could also use sprigs of rosehips or ivy. Attach a length of thin white ribbon or baker's twine to the top of the wreath so you can hang it.

**hint** If you want to hang this as a Christmas decoration you could add several jingle bells in between the hearts.

# CHAPTER 2

# summer
THE FIRST SCENT OF FRESHLY CUT GRASS SIGNALS THE BEGINNING OF SUMMER FOR ME. THAT AROMA, TOGETHER WITH THE SHOUTS OF CHILDREN PLAYING OUTSIDE, SAYS IT ALL. WARM SUNSHINE PUTS A SMILE ON EVERYONE'S FACE AS WE LINGER LONGER OUTSIDE AND CHAT TO PASSERS-BY. THE GARDEN IS TENDED WITH LOVING CARE AND THE FIREPIT WELCOMES YOU TO SIT AND STAY AWHILE. THE PORCH IS DECORATED AND FILLED WITH BUCKETS OF FRESH POSIES THAT ARE SO PLENTIFUL NOW. THOUGHTS TURN TO SANDY BEACHES, WATCHING WAVES CRASHING AND HEARING THE HELLO FROM THE SEAGULLS. THE LAPPING OF WATER AGAINST A SHORELINE IS SUCH A RELAXING SOUND, RELEASING THE STRESSES AND STRAINS OF EVERYDAY LIFE. CREATING THIS SUMMER HOLIDAY MOOD WITHIN YOUR HOME IS EASY TO DO BY ADDING A NEW CUSHION OR SEASIDE DECORATIVE ITEM THAT WILL INSPIRE YOU TO RELAX AND DREAM. THE PROJECTS IN THIS CHAPTER ARE DESIGNED TO BRING SUMMER INTO YOUR HOME, EVEN IF YOUR HOLIDAY IS WEEKS AWAY.

# driftwood heart

NOTHING SAYS SEASIDE BETTER THAN BLEACHED PIECES OF DRIFTWOOD. THEY CONJURE UP IMAGES OF STORMY SEAS AND WILD WAVES AND DELIVER A MESSAGE OF MYSTERY TO THE SHORE, LEAVING THE FINDER OF SUCH TREASURE TO CREATE A LASTING IMAGE TO TAKE HOME. THE DRIFTWOOD SHOWN HERE WAS FOUND ON THE SHORES OF LAKE HURON IN CANADA AND IS A CONSTANT REMINDER OF HAPPY CHILDHOOD SUMMERS SPENT IN MY BEAUTIFUL HOMETOWN OF KINCARDINE, ONTARIO.

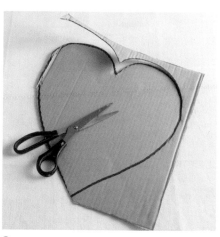

**1** Using a marker pen and the template on page 116, draw the shape of a heart on a piece of cardboard to the size you would like.

**2** Cut out the heart shape with scissors.

## MATERIALS

Cardboard (ideally reuse from a box or some packaging)

Marker pen

Small pieces of driftwood

String

## TOOLS

Template on page 116

Scissors

Hot glue gun

**3** Start adding pieces of driftwood to the heart shape, starting with the outline of the heart, and glue them in place with the hot glue gun. It's important to fill in all the gaps so that no cardboard shows through. You will probably need more driftwood than you think to make it look three-dimensional.

**4** Cut a short length of string and attach as a loop to the back of the heart with the glue gun so that it lies flat against the wall. Let your imagination soar as you look upon your riches from the seashore!

# tea-light lighthouse

LIGHTHOUSES ARE DOTTED ALL ALONG THE NORDIC COASTLINE AND THE WELCOMING LIGHT SIGNALS TO SAILORS AND VISITORS ALIKE, BRINGING WARMTH AND COMFORT TO ALL. CANDLES AND TEA LIGHTS FEATURE REGULARLY IN SCANDINAVIAN HOMES SO WHAT BETTER WAY TO BRING SOME SCANDI STYLE TO YOUR HOME THAN WITH A LIGHTHOUSE THAT IS ALSO USEFUL? THIS PROJECT IS A LITTLE MORE ADVANCED AND IS FOR THOSE WHO FEEL COMFORTABLE WITH WOODWORK—OR WHO HAVE SOMEONE WHO IS HAPPY TO CUT OUT THE SHAPES FOR YOU!

## MATERIALS

Piece of flat wood, approximately ½ in. (1 cm) thick

Doweling

Nails

Thin wire

Small piece of scrap metal

Cream paint

Fabric scraps

Needle and thread

Button (optional)

## TOOLS

Templates on pages 124–125

Pencil and ruler

Fret saw

Hammer

Paintbrush

Scissors

White craft (PVA) glue

**1** Use the templates on pages 124–125 to draw the shapes onto the wood and then cut them out using a fret saw. Cut a short length of dowel for the flagpole and a slightly longer piece for the boat's mast.

**2** Take the semicircle piece (this is the lighthouse balcony) and hammer in five nails, making sure they are evenly spaced.

**3** Wrap two rows of wire around the nails—this creates a little fence around the balcony.

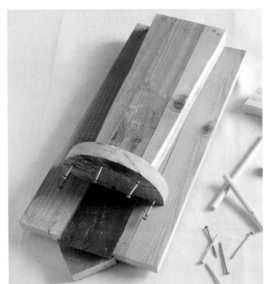

**4** Hammer the small piece of thin scrap metal to the top of the backing wood. This is necessary if you plan to use a real tea light, as it will protect the wood from the flame. Using the photograph as a guide, attach all pieces of wood to the backing wood, including the boat and mast, using a hammer and nails.

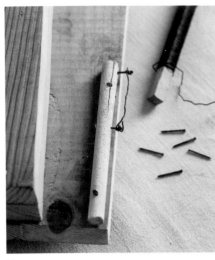

**5** Hammer the flagpole to the right of the lighthouse and then add two more nails and twist some wire between the two.

**6** Paint the lighthouse, boat, and flagpole but be careful not to paint the metal piece.

**7** Cut out small squares of fabric from your scraps and glue them on to the base of the lighthouse using white craft (PVA) glue.

**8** Cut a short length of wire to run from the top of the mast to the boat. Cut small diamond shapes from the fabric scraps, fold them over the wire, and glue in place. Make a small flag for the flagpole in the same way. Cut a triangle of fabric for the sail and attach to the wire with thread (you can make this as decorative as you like, adding a small button or some stitching).

# mending kit—a modern "huswif"

I AM FORTUNATE ENOUGH TO OWN QUITE A FEW OLD EDITIONS OF SCANDINAVIAN BOOKS. MANY OF THE PICTURES ARE OF LADIES AND LITTLE GIRLS SEWING HAPPILY INDOORS OR IN THE GARDEN. BY THEIR SIDE IS EITHER A SEWING BOX OR A LITTLE BAG CONTAINING SEWING ESSENTIALS. THESE DAYS MORE AND MORE PEOPLE ARE RECOGNIZING THE JOY IN REPAIRING THINGS; MY LOVELY FRIEND KAREN CARRIES WITH HER LITTLE POUCHES FILLED WITH MENDING NECESSITIES EVERYWHERE AND ANYWHERE SHE GOES. THIS INSPIRED ME TO MAKE A MENDING KIT. I ADDED A LAVENDER FILLED PINCUSHION, WHICH RELEASES A GORGEOUS AROMA EVERY TIME A PIN IS USED. THE ENTIRE POUCH ATTACHES TO ANY APRON OR SHIRT WITH THE AID OF A BUTTON AND SOME STRING. THERE IS SOMETHING QUITE COMFORTING IN BRINGING THE GOOD IDEAS OF THE PAST INTO PRESENT TIMES.

## MATERIALS

Selection of coordinating fabrics for the pouch and pincushion

Delicate lining fabric for the pouch (optional)

Dried lavender

Ribbon (optional)

Fabric scraps to decorate the bag

Button

Baker's twine

## TOOLS

Scissors

Needle and matching sewing thread

Pins

**1** Start by cutting fabric for the pouch: the finished size is 9 x 8 in. (23 x 20 cm) so cut two rectangles of fabric to these measurements, adding ½ in. (1 cm) all round for seam allowances. Cut two extra rectangles from your lining fabric, if using, and stitch right sides together to each rectangle, leaving a gap for turning through.

**2** Turn the stitched pieces right sides out through the gap and then pin them right sides (outside pieces) together. Stitch around the edges, leaving the top open. Turn out the right way.

**3** Cut two 6½ in. (16 cm) squares of fabric for the pincushion and stitch then right sides together, leaving one side open. Turn right sides out.

**4** Fill the pincushion with dried lavender, pushing it into the corners.

**5** Add a loop of ribbon (or use a scrap of fabric) and insert just inside the gap. Pin in place and then slipstitch the opening closed.

**6** Add any decoration you like to the pouch. I added an old monogram that I have kept for years, knowing that one day I will use it! I also added a small patch of contrasting fabric for decoration.

**7** Add a button to the edge of the pouch—this is so you can attach the pincushion to the pouch with some baker's twine, as well as to attach the pouch to another garment.

# summer tablecloth

SUMMER IN SCANDINAVIA SIGNALS THE RETURN TO THE BELOVED HUTTE (COTTAGES) ON THE MANY ISLANDS DOTTED AROUND THE COAST. THE SUMMER MONTHS ARE FILLED WITH IMPROMPTU MEALS HELD OUTSIDE AND MANY VISITORS POP OVER TO ENJOY THIS SPECIAL TIME. EACH TIME THAT I HAVE BEEN LUCKY ENOUGH TO ENJOY THIS SECLUSION, I HAVE ALWAYS ADMIRED HOW BEAUTIFULLY EVERYTHING IS DECORATED. WINDY DAYS ARE NOT UNCOMMON AND MANY A TIME A STRONG GUST OF WIND WOULD PICK UP THE CORNER OF THE TABLECLOTH AND SPILL SOMETHING. IT IS EASY TO WEIGH DOWN A TABLECLOTH AND THIS IS SUCH A SIMPLE THING TO MAKE YOURSELF, MAKING IT A WONDERFUL HOSTESS GIFT.

**1** Measure out your checked fabric to the size you need for your table. Be sure to leave enough fabric to hang over the table—a drop of 8–10 in. (20–25 cm) is ideal so add twice this to the dimensions of the table to get your fabric size. (You could also use an existing tablecloth.) Cut four triangles from the plain fabric for the corners of the tablecloth—the short edges should be approximately 5 in. (12.5 cm).

## MATERIALS

Checked linen fabric for the tablecloth

Plain linen fabric for the corner pockets

4 buttons

Ribbon

Stones

## TOOLS

Tape measure

Scissors

Needle and matching sewing thread

Pins

**2** Hem all four sides of the checked fabric, as well as the longest edge of each triangle. With right sides together, pin each triangle to the tablecloth fabric then sew the two smaller edges of each triangle to the tablecloth edges, leaving the long edge of the triangle open. Turn the triangles right side out.

**3** Take one button for each triangle and sew it onto the center of the long edge of each triangle.

**4** Cut four lengths of ribbon, each 10 in. (25 cm) long. Fold each length of ribbon in half and stitch the center point to the tablecloth fabric, just inside the triangle (you should not be able to see the ribbon when it is sewn). When you have laid the tablecloth on the table place a large stone inside each triangle pocket and tie the ribbons around the buttons. The weight at each corner will keep the cloth flat so no amount of wind will disrupt your dinner!

# wedding bunting
NOTHING SAYS CELEBRATION BETTER THAN ROW UPON ROW OF BUNTING FLUTTERING IN THE BREEZE—IT IS AN ESTABLISHED FORM OF DECORATION IN MOST COUNTRIES. WEDDINGS PRESENT SO MUCH SCOPE FOR THE IMAGINATION WHEN PONDERING OVER DECOR. MANY BRIDAL COUPLES WANT TO PROVIDE A SMALL TOKEN OF APPRECIATION TO THOSE WHO HAVE TAKEN THE TIME TO COME TO THEIR WEDDING, WHICH IS WHERE THIS CHARMING

PROJECT COMES IN. THE LITTLE FLORAL POUCHES PROVIDE DECORATION DURING THE EVENT AND THEN ACT AS TAKE-HOME PRESENTS AS THE GUESTS LEAVE. THEY ARE SIMPLY TOLD TO REMOVE THE PEG THAT HOLDS THE POUCH AND TAKE IT AWAY WITH THEM. THEY CAN BE FILLED WITH FLOWERS, SWEETS OR SOME OTHER OFFERING AS A MEMORY OF THE DAY. SIMPLY MADE, YET FILLED WITH THE WARMTH AND LOVE THAT ONLY HAND-MADE CAN PROVIDE.

**1** Using the template on page 121, draw as many bunting shapes as you need onto your quilt scraps, then cut them out.

**2** Fold over the top of each bunting piece and stitch along close to the fabric edge to create a small channel. Thread the bunting onto a length of cord or ribbon.

## MATERIALS

Old quilt scraps

Cord or ribbon

Floral fabric scraps

Wooden pegs

## TOOLS

Templates on page 121

Pencil

Scissors

Needle and matching sewing thread

**3** Collect several different floral fabrics to create a variety of pouches of different shapes and sizes. You can use the templates on page 121 or cut them freehand. By not having a uniform shape the bunting is so much more interesting and pleasing to the eye.

**4** Cut out your shapes and sew them right sides together, leaving the top open. It is also lovely to stitch different floral fabrics together in a patchwork —this way you can use up even small fabric scraps. Turn them right side out and press neatly. They are now ready to be pegged onto the triangles and filled with your choice of present.

# boat in a box

SAILING IS A FAVORITE PASTIME FOR MANY PEOPLE, NOT LEAST THE SCANDINAVIANS. FROM LITTLE ROWBOATS TO HUGE YACHTS, THEIR LOVE OF THE SEA RUNS DEEP IN THEIR VEINS. IT IS NOT SURPRISING THEN TO FIND MANY SHIP MODELS AND SEAFARING PICTURES DECORATING NORTHERN EUROPEAN HOMES. THIS BOAT IN A BOX IS A FUN PROJECT THAT CAN INVOLVE ALL THE FAMILY. GATHER ODD SCRAPS OF RIBBON AND FABRIC TOGETHER, FIND SOMEONE WITH SOME BASIC WOODWORK SKILLS AND YOU WILL HAVE YOURSELF A JOLLY AFTERNOON CREATING.

## MATERIALS

Piece of wood, about 1½ in. (4 cm) thick

Shallow box

Dowel

Small eye screws

Wire

Fabric scraps

Ribbon scraps

Quilt scrap

Buttons

## TOOLS

Templates on page 115

Pencil

Jigsaw

Hand drill

Wire cutters

Scissors

White craft (PVA) glue

Needle and matching sewing thread

**1** Use the template on page 115 to draw the boat shape onto your piece of wood (you can scale it up or down to fit your chosen box) and then cut it out using the jigsaw. Drill a small hole in the top for the mast (dowel) and push it into place.

**2** Twist the small eye screws into the wood at either end of the top of the boat and then add one to the top of the mast. Cut a length of wire and loop it through all three eyes. Twist the ends back over the wire to secure.

**3** Start decorating the boat by glueing on scraps of fabric and ribbons. To make the bunting, fold a scrap of fabric in half and draw small triangles along the fold line. Cut out the triangles (except the side that's on the fold) so you get a sort of "diamond" shape. Apply glue to one side and then fold over the mast wire.

**4** Cut a sail from the quilt scrap using the template on page 115. Using a blanket stitch (see page 108), stitch around the sail edges. Sew on some patches and a button decoration, then stitch three buttons to each corner of the sail, leaving a long thread tail at each corner. Use these threads to attach the sail to the screw eyes on the boat. Sit your boat in the box as if ready to set sail. Be careful… you may feel like creating a whole fleet once you start!

# nautical patchwork pillows

I HAVE BEEN FORTUNATE ENOUGH TO HAVE EXPERIENCED SUMMER IN SWEDEN WITH FRIENDS ON THEIR ISLAND. HAVING A LITTLE COTTAGE (HUTTE) ON THE OCEAN IS THE WAY MANY SPEND THEIR SUMMERS. IT IS A CAREFREE WAY OF LIFE: SIMPLE PLEASURES SUCH AS FRESH FOOD, BONFIRES, BOATING, READING, AND, MOST IMPORTANTLY, SPENDING TIME TOGETHER, TAKE UP MOST OF THE DAYS. ELECTRICITY IS NOT ALWAYS AVAILABLE BUT THE HOME COMFORTS OF WARM BLANKETS AND COMFORTABLE PILLOWS ARE PLENTIFUL. FINDING RED, WHITE, AND BLUE FABRICS DEPICTING MARITIME AND NAUTICAL LIFE CAN ONLY ADD TO THE SPARKLE OF SUMMER.

## MATERIALS

Selection of red, white, and blue fabrics that look pleasing together.

16 in. (40 cm) pillow pad

## TOOLS

Tape measure

Scissors

Needle and matching sewing thread

**1** Gather together your fabrics and decide how you want to arrange your patchwork, using the photograph opposite as a guide. You need to create two squares of fabric (for the front and back of the pillow) that are 17 x 17 in. (42 x 42 cm) square; this allows for a ½ in. (1 cm) seam allowance around the outer edges. Remember to leave a ¼ in. (0.5 cm) seam allowance for attaching the smaller squares together.

**2** In this project, the front of the square pillow has a central square, four smaller squares at each corner, two strips at the top and bottom, and a strip of ten small squares and one small rectangle at each side of the pillow. Each small square measures 2 x 2 in. (5 x 5 cm) and the small rectangle measures 4 x 2 in. (10 x 5 cm). Sew the squares together in pairs with the rectangle at one end, leaving a ¼ in. (0.5 cm) seam allowance. Lay the fabric pieces together as shown and stitch one side at a time, right sides together. Press the seams open.

**hint** Use any leftover pieces of fabric to make a few more pillows to create a very cozy corner.

**3** Put the front and back pieces right sides together and sew around the edges with a ½ in. (1 cm) seam allowance, leaving a gap at one end to insert the pillow pad.

**4** Trim the seam allowances and turn the pillow cover right sides out, making sure you push out the corners. Insert the pillow pad and then slipstitch (see page 107) the opening closed.

# framed lighthouse stitchery

I AM NEVER ONE TO THROW AWAY ANY USABLE SCRAP OF FABRIC, RIBBON, OR STRING AND THIS IS AN EXAMPLE OF A PROJECT THAT HAS BEEN DESIGNED WITH JUST THOSE SCRAPS IN MIND. WHENEVER I SEE A WORKING LIGHTHOUSE AN AIR OF MYSTERY ENVELOPS ME. IT MAY BE BECAUSE OF ALL THE BOOKS I HAVE READ, BUT HEARING A FOGHORN, SEEING A DENSE MIST HUGGING THE SHORELINE, AND THEN GLIMPSING THE WELCOMING WARM BEAMS OF A LIGHTHOUSE FILLS ME WITH IMMENSE COMFORT. IT IS NOT SURPRISING THAT I LOVE TO DECORATE MY HOME IN THE SUMMER WITH PICTURES OF THESE ICONS. HISTORICALLY LIGHTHOUSES WERE VERY IMPORTANT TO SCANDINAVIAN MARINERS AS THE NORTH ATLANTIC CURRENTS WERE TREACHEROUS. I CAN JUST IMAGINE THEIR RELIEF WHEN THEY SIGHTED THIS GUIDING RADIANCE.

## MATERIALS

Old wooden frame (look in thrift stores or yard sales)

Linen fabric slightly larger than your frame

Red, white, and blue fabric scraps

Ribbon

Embroidery floss (thread)

Piece of cardboard

Pieces of wood for the boat and mast

Cream paint (I used water-based eggshell)

Screw-in hook and eye

Wire

Button

## TOOLS

Scissors

Vanishing fabric pen

Template on page 118

White craft (PVA) glue

Needle

Staple gun

Hot glue gun

Fret saw

Paintbrush

**1** Gather your fabrics, ribbon, and embroidery floss (thread) together, choosing colors and patterns that will complement each other. Use a fabric pen to mark out the area that will show in the frame so you know to keep the design within these lines.

**2** Using the photograph as a guide, cut scraps of fabric to make up the body of the lighthouse and glue these in position. Using the template on page 118 and a fabric pen, copy the compass design onto the linen (the marks from the pen will disappear in a few days). Using two strands of embroidery floss (thread), embroider the compass design, using backstitch and chain stitch (see pages 108 and 110). Add further details to the lighthouse using running stitch, backstitch, cross stitch, and satin stitch and embroider some flying seagulls in the sky. When your stitchery is complete, attach it to a piece of cardboard that is the same size as the frame: fold the edges of the stitchery around the cardboard and attach with a staple gun (you could also use a glue gun or some tape).

**3** Make the little boat and mast—these can be made from wood or thick cardboard. If using wood, carefully use a fret saw to cut out a small shape of a boat. The mast can be any piece of wood dowel that you may have. Paint both pieces and allow to dry.

**4** Using a hot glue gun, attach the little boat and the mast to the frame.

**5** Screw a hook to the top of the mast and an eye to the boat and twist a short length of wire around them so you can add the flag bunting. Cut small diamond shapes from the fabric scraps, fold them over the wire, and glue in place with white craft (PVA) glue (this will make the bunting stiff so it looks like it's flying in the wind). Add ribbon and a button to finish off the little boat.

**6** When everything is stitched and secured, use a staple gun to attach your stitchery to the frame. Finally attach a ribbon to the back of the frame so you can hang your stitchery.

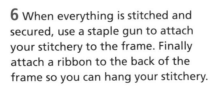

# Child's stool

SEASIDE ADVENTURES OCCUR YEAR ROUND IN SCANDINAVIA; WHATEVER THE WEATHER, THE SEA IN ALL ITS GLORY IS ADMIRED, RESPECTED, AND ENJOYED. A COASTAL BACKDROP TO DECORATE A CHILD'S ROOM IS A POPULAR THEME. MY SON RECEIVED THIS LITTLE VINTAGE STOOL WHEN HE WAS ABOUT THREE YEARS OLD; IT FOLDS SO IT IS VERY EASY TO CARRY AROUND FOR A LITTLE ONE. HE TOOK IT FROM ROOM TO ROOM, INSIDE AND OUT. IT CERTAINLY DELIGHTED HIM FOR A LONG TIME. IT HAS BEEN FOLDED UP, SITTING RATHER FORLORNLY IN A CORNER FOR TWENTY-FOUR YEARS. I GLANCED AT IT AND DECIDED THERE AND THEN IT NEEDED A NEW LOOK. I SEARCHED MY FABRIC STASH FOR JUST THE RIGHT MATERIAL AND ADDED A LITTLE POCKET TO HANG FROM THE STOOL SO THAT TREASURES COULD BE TRANSPORTED AS WELL. WHO KNOWS, ONE DAY ANOTHER LITTLE ONE MAY HAVE FUN WITH IT!

## MATERIALS

Old folding stool (look in thrift stores or at vintage fairs)

Fabric

Small upholstery tacks or nails

Ribbon

## TOOLS

Scissors

Needle and matching sewing thread or sewing machine

Hammer

**1** Gather your fabrics for the seat cover and the pocket. Measure the seat area and decide how much you need to add to the width to allow for attaching the fabric to the stool. Cut the seat fabric to these measurements, adding ½ in. (1 cm) all around for the hem. Decide how big you want the pocket to be and cut a piece of fabric that is double the height.

**2** Turn a ½ in. (1 cm) hem over to the wrong side of the seat fabric and stitch in place, either by hand using backstitch (see page 108) or with a sewing machine. For the pocket simply fold the fabric in half wrong sides together and stitch the two side seams with a ½ in. (1 cm) seam allowance.

**3** Attach the fabric to fit the stool with some small black nails so that the fabric is secure. The more little nails that you add, the more secure the fabric will be on the stool.

**4** Stitch a hem around the top edge of the pocket. Cut two small loops of ribbon and attach them to the pocket so that they can loop over the ends of the stool. Turn the pocket right side out.

# CHAPTER 3

## fall

IN ONE OF MY FAVORITE CHILDHOOD BOOKS, 'ANNE OF GREEN GABLES', ANNE SAYS, "I'M SO GLAD I LIVE IN A WORLD WHERE THERE ARE OCTOBERS". I COULD NOT AGREE MORE. THE RICH COLORS OF FALL (AUTUMN) COMBINED WITH LEAVES DANCING IN THE WIND AND WOOD SMOKE FILLING THE AIR BRINGS SUCH A CONTENTED FEELING OF HYGGE. THE CRUNCHING SOUND OF WALKING ALONG A PATH STREWN WITH FALLEN APPLES, TWIGS, AND GLISTENING CHESTNUTS MINGLES WITH CRIES FROM THE CROWS. THE BUSY SCURRYING OF LITTLE ANIMALS GEARING UP FOR WINTER SIGNALS TO ALL TO MAKE SURE THAT THE WOODPILE IS REPLENISHED AND READY FOR THAT FIRST FROST. WARM, THICK WOOL SWEATERS FILL UP THE CUPBOARDS AND BLANKETS AND QUILTS COVER SOFAS AND CHAIRS, INVITING YOU TO RELAX. ENERGY IS RENEWED AFTER THE HEAT OF THE SUMMER AND THE STIRRINGS OF CREATIVITY BEGINS. TO ME, NOTHING IS NICER THAN STITCHING BY AN OPEN FIRE OR GATHERING A COLLECTION OF HARVEST BOUNTY TO MAKE A WREATH FOR MY FRONT DOOR. THE PROJECTS IN THIS CHAPTER WILL ENTICE YOU TO CREATE A COMFORTING NEST IN YOUR HOME TO EMBRACE THIS RESPLENDENT SEASON.

# autumn welcome

IN SCANDINAVIA THE CHANGE OF SEASONS IS A CAUSE FOR CELEBRATION. THE EXCITEMENT OF THE NEXT SEASON IS FUELLED BY THE CHANGING LIGHT, DANCING LEAVES, AND FRESH SHOOTS THAT APPEAR AS IF BY MAGIC. WE CAN MIRROR THESE CHANGES BY DECORATING OUR HOMES TO REFLECT THE SEASON. THIS PROJECT CAN BE ALTERED TO REFLECT ANY SEASON, A SIMPLE YET EYE-CATCHING CREATION TO EMBRACE ANOTHER NEW TIME OF YEAR.

## MATERIALS

Selection of fabrics in autumnal colors

Fusible bonding web

Piece of wood for the sign

Wire

Rusted metal embellishments for decoration

## TOOLS

Iron

Pencil

Scissors

White craft (PVA) glue

Paintbrush

**1** Gather all your fabrics together and decide which fabric should be for each letter. Iron the fusible bonding web to the wrong side of the fabric pieces, following the manufacturer's instructions.

**2** Draw out the letters onto the fusible bonding web, remembering to reverse the shapes. Cut each one out. The fusible bonding web makes the fabric stiff and also stops it from fraying.

**3** Glue the letters onto the wood with white craft (PVA) glue. Press them down firmly and leave to dry.

**4** Take a long length of wire (at least twice the length of your piece of wood) and wrap the ends around the wood. Add on any metal embellishments you may have, securing them with wire. Rosehips and leaves would also look lovely.

# picket fence post holder

HOW MANY OF US PICK UP THE POST FROM THE FLOOR AND POP IT DOWN ANYWHERE, ONLY TO FIND IT DAYS LATER? HAVING A DESIGNATED SPOT TO HOLD ALL THE MAIL NOT ONLY LOOKS PRETTY BUT SOLVES MANY HARASSED MOMENTS WHEN HUNTING FOR LOST LETTERS. FOR THOSE WITH LIMITED SPACE THIS WHIMSICAL WALL-HUNG LETTER HOLDER, WITH ITS PICKET FENCE AND BUNTING, IS DECORATIVE AS WELL AS USEFUL.

## MATERIALS

4 pieces of wood for the frame, each 21 x 2.5 in. (55 x 6 cm)

14 in. (36 cm) square piece of backing board

Piece of wood (for the base of the picket fence), 11 in. (28 cm) long

Approximately 9 "pickets" (mine came from a broken crate), each 5 x 1 in. (13 x 2.5 cm)

Nails

Paint (I use water-based eggshell)

Wire

Fabric scraps

Decorative paper

Screws

## TOOLS

Hammer

Paintbrush

Wire cutters

Scissors

White craft (PVA) glue

**1** Gather all your wooden pieces together. Construct the frame with the four identical pieces. Be sure to overlap the wood strips to make it look whimsical.

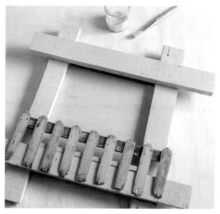

**2** Next nail the backing board to the back of the frame. Add the small piece of wood for the base of the picket fence—this is so that the letters don't fall through the gap in the frame. Finally add the pickets by nailing them to the frame. Paint all the pieces the same color and allow to dry. Add a second coat if needed, although I like to leave the pickets with a slightly rough finish.

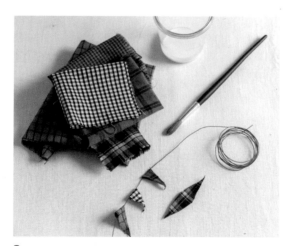

**3** Cut a length of wire to fit across the picket fence. To make the bunting, fold a scrap of fabric in half and draw small triangles along the fold line. Cut out the triangles (except the side that's on the fold) so you get a sort of "diamond" shape. Apply a blob of glue to one side of the fabric and then fold over the wire. Using a lot of glue will secure the bunting and, once dry, will stiffen the fabric so the bunting hangs sweetly.

**4** Glue the decorative backing to the backing board. Add two screws to the back of the frame and add wire for hanging (twist fabric around the wire if you like). Finally, add the bunting by twisting the wire around the end pickets. The bunting gives the frame a seasonal twist—why not change it with the seasons?

# sweet sampler scrap pelmet

I CAN OFTEN BE FOUND RUMMAGING THROUGH BEAUTIFUL BUNDLES OF FABRIC AT VINTAGE FAIRS. I LOVE HOW THESE OLD SCRAPS TELL A STORY AND I CAN NEVER, EVER THROW ANY AWAY. RECENTLY, I BOUGHT A RATHER BADLY TORN OLD PILLOWCASE—I SAW THE INTRICATE WORK ON THE EMBROIDERY AND COULD NOT PASS IT BY. I CAREFULLY WASHED IT AND LOOKED AT WHAT COULD BE SALVAGED. ON CLOSER INSPECTION I FOUND A SMALL, BEAUTIFULLY EMBROIDERED CROWN WITH THE DATE 1859. I FELT LIKE I HAD WON THE LOTTERY! THIS LITTLE PILLOWCASE MUST HAVE BEEN IN USE IN THE ROYAL HOUSEHOLD. I HAD A SIMILAR EXPERIENCE WITH THIS FABRIC. THE NAME AND DATES WERE STILL INTACT AND HOME IT CAME WITH ME, TO BE CLEANED AND THEN REPURPOSED AS A SMALL PELMET IN MY KITCHEN, WHERE I ADMIRE IT EVERY DAY AND WONDER ABOUT THE YOUNG GIRL, EDITH DIX, WHO CREATED IT IN 1901.

## MATERIALS

Sampler scrap

Tea towel

Cafe curtain wire

Hook and eyes

## TOOLS

Scissors

Needle and matching sewing thread

**1** Find a tea towel that matches the sampler fabric scrap and cut it to size to fit a small window. A slight gather is very nice, but to be able to read the sampler, it will need to be almost flat against the window.

**2** Fold the top of the tea towel over to the wrong side by 1 in. (2.5 cm) and sew across the fabric to make a casing for the cafe curtain wire.

**3** Position the sampler piece on top of the tea towel and stitch in place.

**4** Take the cafe curtain wire with a hook at either end and thread it through the casing. Screw the corresponding eyes to the top of the window frame and attach your sweet little pelmet.

# fall wreath

AFTER I SPENT A DAY LAST YEAR CUTTING BACK MY GRAPEVINE, THE LONG VINES WERE CURLED UPON MY LAWN LOOKING RATHER FORLORN. OVER A CUP OF TEA AN IDEA STRUCK… WREATHS ARE MADE FROM GRAPEVINE… I MUST CREATE AS MANY AS I CAN FROM THIS HARVEST. I QUICKLY GATHERED ALL THE LENGTHS OF VINE AND SOAKED THEM OVERNIGHT TO MAKE THEM MORE PLIABLE. WREATHS GIVE ALL WHO SEE THEM A WARM WELCOME AND PLAY AN IMPORTANT ROLE IN THE SCANDINAVIAN HOME. EVERY SEASON GIVES CAUSE TO CREATE A NEW WREATH—A FALL CIRCLET OF BERRIES, ROSEHIPS, OAK LEAVES, AND HYDRANGEAS IS GORGEOUS AND LONG-LASTING AND IS EASIER TO MAKE THAN YOU MIGHT THINK.

## MATERIALS

Grapevine

Florist's wire

Rosehips

Blackberry branches (the berries can be green, red, or black)

Hydrangeas

Oak leaves (with acorns attached)

Linen fabric

## TOOLS

Secateurs

Scissors

**1** Decide on the size of your wreath—the one pictured is 23 in. (55 cm) in diameter. Gather together as many lengths of grapevine as you think you need and start shaping them into a wreath, attaching the lengths by twisting with florist's wire. The more you have the thicker it will be.

**2** Start by attaching bunches of rosehips and blackberry branches first. Make a bundle of each, securing the bundle with wire, and then attach each bundle to the grapevine.

**3** Add the hydrangea blooms, acorns, and oak leaves with wire to fill out the bottom half of the wreath. I like to leave the top half of the wreath free of any decoration.

**4** Finally, cut a length of linen fabric to be tied in a bow at the top of the wreath. I find that the linen hangs beautifully and adds a sophisticated elegance to a rustic wreath.

# frieda the friendly witch

HALLOWEEN IS A DELIGHTFUL WELCOME TO THE FALL SEASON. ALL OF A SUDDEN, COLORS CHANGE FROM PINK AND GREEN TO ORANGE AND BLACK. WREATHS OF COLORFUL LEAVES DECORATE FRONT DOORS, PORCHES ARE ADORNED WITH CORN STALKS, AND THE CHEERFUL PUMPKIN GETS THE HONOR IT'S DUE. FOR ME HALLOWEEN IS ALWAYS A TIME OF FRIVOLITY, WHICH IS EXACTLY WHY MY LITTLE WITCH IS EXTREMELY FRIENDLY.

## MATERIALS

Selection of fabrics in coordinating colors

Toy stuffing or cotton balls

String

Black felt for the hat

Spanish moss for her hair

Thin sticks

Fabric pen

Putka seed pods (or use acorns, small chestnuts or whole spices)

Wire

## TOOLS

Templates on page 119

Scissors

Needle and matching sewing thread

Sewing machine (optional)

Safety pin

Glue gun

**1** Gather all the material needed for the project. Decide what fabric you want for the body and use the template on page 119 to cut two triangle body shapes. Cut two pieces of fabric for her head. Sew each head piece to a body piece right sides together, with a ½ in. (1 cm) seam allowance, then sew the two pieces right sides together, again with a ½ in. (1 cm) seam allowance. (You can stitch by hand or use a sewing machine.) Remember to leave a gap at the top where you will stuff the body.

**2** Using toy stuffing or cotton balls, stuff the body and head quite tightly. Sew the gap shut.

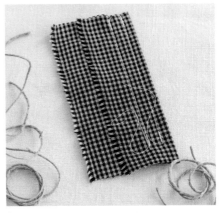

**3** To make the witch's apron cut a piece of fabric that is 10 x 6 in. (25 x 15 cm). Fold the fabric over (by how much depends how long you want the apron to be) and stitch two rows of stitching about ½ in. (1 cm) from the folded edge to create a channel. Do not sew the seams of the apron—the fraying edge of the material adds to her appearance. Attach a safety pin to a length of string and thread it through the channel, then pull to gather up the apron.

**4** Cut a piece of fabric for the cape that is 16 x 8 in. (40 x 20 cm). Fold 1½ in. (4 cm) over to the wrong side and stitch a channel, as described above. Thread through a piece of string and pull to gather.

**5** The hat is easy and fun to make. Use the template on page 119 to cut two triangles from black felt. Sew the triangles together down the long sides to make a cone shape and turn inside out. Then use the template to to cut an oval shape for the hat brim. Cut two snips into the oval shape in the form of a cross—take care not to make the snips too large—and insert the triangle through the hole made by the snips. Use a glue gun to keep it in place.

**6** Tie on the apron then the cape. Attach as much Spanish moss as you want for her hair using the glue gun. When you are happy with the hair, attach the hat with the glue gun

**7** Attach two sticks for the arms and two for legs with the glue gun. Make sure the arms stick out enough to hold the garland you will make. Using your fabric pen, draw on two eyes.

**8** Make the garland. I've used putka seed pods as they look like mini pumpkins. Twist a length of wire around the pods and then attach the garland to the witch's arms. Frieda is now ready to fly to the delight of all!

# quick idea BOWL OF TWINE

Nothing is nicer than looking at all one's collections and realizing that just by changing a ribbon or adding some fabric a new and beautiful decorative item can be created. I was busy one morning switching my living room from summer to fall when I came upon a basket full of balls of twine—they looked pretty as they were. But I had just folded up a lovely mound of homespun fabric and, looking at the fabric, I tore up several lengths. The fabric strips now feature around the balls of twine, mingled with bright orange mini pumpkins. The whole bowl now just says Fall. It only took a few minutes to make with random things I had stored in my cupboard. I hope this will entice you to rediscover things you already have tucked away out of sight that can actually be made into something wonderful.

## MATERIALS

Balls of twine

Homespun fabric

Mini pumpkins

## TOOLS

Scissors

**1** Tear or cut several lengths of homespun fabric into approximately 10 in. (25 cm) lengths.

**2** Tie one length around each ball of twine.

**3** Arrange in a bowl and scatter with mini pumpkins.

# pumpkin pillow

GROWING UP IN CANADA I WITNESSED FOUR DISTINCT SEASONS. MY MOTHER FOLLOWED THE SEASONAL CHANGES BY CHANGING THE DECOR AT HOME. CURTAINS WOULD CHANGE IN SOME ROOMS, RUGS WOULD BE ROLLED OUT OR UP, PILLOWS RECOVERED, AND FLOWER VASES WOULD SHOWCASE THE SEASONAL SPLENDOR. THIS LEFT A HUGE IMPRESSION ON ME—I AM ALWAYS TAKING A CUE FROM NATURE TO TELL ME WHEN IT IS TIME TO CHANGE THE INTERIOR. PILLOWS ARE SUCH AN EASY AND QUICK WAY TO REDECORATE.

**1** Cut a 12 in. (30 cm) square of fabric for the back of the pillow. Cut four strips for the front, each 12 x 2.5 in. (30 x 6 cm). Cut a piece for the center panel that is 12 x 7 in. (30 x 18 cm). Now cut several squares of fabric for the center pumpkin. Don't worry about making the squares too uniform as pumpkins are all different sizes and shapes; in fact, I think it looks much more interesting if they are slightly wonky and free-flowing. Stitch the squares right sides together, by hand or with a sewing machine, then iron the fabric and cut it into strips.

## MATERIALS

Selection of wool fabrics in different autumnal hues

Fusible bonding web

Green embroidery floss (thread)

13 in. (33 cm) square pillow pad

## TOOLS

Scissors

Needle and matching sewing thread

Sewing machine (optional)

Iron

Template on page 122

Friction pen

Maple leaf cookie cutter (optional)

**2** Sew the strips together to make one large piece of patchwork fabric. Following the manufacturer's instructions, iron the fusible bonding web onto the back of the patchwork fabric. Using the template on page 122, draw a pumpkin and pumpkin stem onto the bonding web and cut out the shapes. I like to add something to the back of the cushion too so here I have added a maple leaf as a nod to Canada. Using a maple leaf cookie cutter, draw and cut out the leaf. Iron the pumpkin to the front of the center panel and the maple leaf to the back panel.

**3** Using two strands of green embroidery floss (thread), blanket stitch around the pumpkin and stem (see page 108). Embroider some vine tendrils around the base of the stem using stem stitch (see page 111).

**4** With the fabric right sides together and with a ½ in. (1 cm) seam allowance, stitch the two strips of wool fabric for the front to either side of the pumpkin center section to create one piece for the front. With right sides together sew the two wool fabric pieces together with a ½ in. (1 cm) seam allowance. Remember to leave a gap for turning and inserting the pillow.

**5** Turn the pillow cover out the right way and push out the corners. Insert the pillow pad and then slipstitch the gap closed (see page 107).

# foraging basket

FALL (AUTUMN) IS A TIME FOR GATHERING IN THE HARVEST, WHILE FESTIVALS ARE CELEBRATED IN MANY TOWNS AND VILLAGES AND PEOPLE GIVE THANKS FOR NATURE'S ABUNDANCE. NEIGHBORS SHARE THEIR BOUNTY WITH FRIENDS AND FAMILY AND BASKETS ARE COLLECTED FOR THE LESS FORTUNATE TO ENJOY. I LOVE SEEING PRODUCE BY THE ROADSIDE NEATLY PACKAGED WITH AN HONESTY BOX ON THE TABLE. OFTEN THERE ARE BASKETS OF APPLES FREE FOR THE TAKING, PERFECT FOR MAKING WARM CINNAMON APPLE CIDER TO KEEP THE CHILL IN THE AIR AT BAY. IN SCANDINAVIA, THE ANNUAL HUNT FOR EDIBLE MUSHROOMS IS AN AGE-OLD TRADITION ON THE CALENDAR. A BOOK EXPLAINING WHICH MUSHROOMS ARE SAFE IS PLACED IN THE FORAGING BASKET ALONG WITH A SMALL BRUSH TO CLEAN THEM. LATER, WHEN THE MUSHROOMS ARE COLLECTED, A DELICIOUS MEAL WILL BE PRODUCED AND ALL WILL BE ASTOUNDED AT WHAT NATURE PROVIDES. OF COURSE, THIS FORAGING BASKET CAN BE USED TO GATHER ALL SORTS OF WILD AND WONDERFUL THINGS... IT'S UP TO YOU!

## MATERIALS

Basket

Selection of fabric squares and strips

Scrap of linen fabric

Embroidery floss (thread) in light brown, dark brown, white, and green

Linen backing fabric, approximately 20 x 16 in. (50 x 40 cm)

## TOOLS

Scissors

Sewing machine or needle and matching sewing thread

Template on page 114

Washable fabric pen

Pins

**1** Gather together your fabric scraps. I used finished antique quilt squares but squares of any fabric to make up a patchwork cover will be fine. For this basket, which is 14 x 7 in. (36 x 18 cm), I used six 5½ in. (14 cm) quilt squares. You'll also need three fabric strips to join up the squares, each one 5½ x 2 in. (14 x 5 cm), and four strips that are 13 x 2 in. (33 x 5 cm). Start by attaching a quilt square to a short strip by stitching right sides together with a ½ in. (1 cm) seam allowance. Attach another quilt square to the other side of the strip in the same way. Repeat until you have three panels each with two quilt squares. Use two of longer fabric strips to attach the three panels so you end up with all six quilt squares joined together. Stitch the remaining two strips to each end of the panel.

**2** Cut two more strips of fabric for the long edges, each 25 x 2 in. (62 x 5 cm). Stitch these to the panel, remembering to sew right sides together with a ½ in. (1 cm) seam allowance. At one corner attach a small piece of linen fabric to the basket cover that is 2 x 2 in. (5 x 5 cm). This is best done by hand: sew right sides together and leave a very small seam allowance. Press it flat then use your fabric pen and the template on page 114 to draw a mushroom onto the square. Using two strands of light brown embroidery floss (thread) fill in the mushroom with long satin stitches (see page 109). Add the dark brown for texture here and there, random white spots on the mushroom, and long green stitches for the grass beside the mushroom stalk.

**3** Cut a piece of linen for the backing fabric that is slightly larger all round than the quilt top. Pin right sides together and stitch around the edges with a ½ in. (1 cm) seam allowance, leaving a small opening to turn the cover right way out.

**4** Trim away any excess fabric from the seams, turn out the right way and slipstitch (see page 107) the gap shut. Give the little cover a good press and you are ready to go foraging.

When there is a chill in the air and the leaves begin to fall, I know it is time to open my trunk full of treasured autumn collections. As soon as I open the lid the sweet scent of cinnamon greets me and I am dazzled by the rich colors before me. I love the tradition of decorating for October 31st but I am the first one to say that I favor a more cozy rather than scary Halloween. Warm wool blankets in orange and brown begin to be dotted about along with pumpkins and the odd witch's hat. I gather armfuls of hydrangeas that dry so beautifully now and place them everywhere. This gave me the idea to make some posy sticks with a bewitching flavor. Simple to make and fun to do with children, they enhance any bouquet and add just the right touch of Halloween magic to your home.

## MATERIALS

Black cardstock

Selection of fabrics and felt

Wooden skewers

Glitter (optional)

## TOOLS

Templates on page 120

Pencil

Cookie cutters (optional)

Scissors

White craft (PVA) glue

**1** Using the templates on page 120 and a pencil, draw your shapes onto the black cardstock. You will need two shapes for each stick. Alternatively you can draw around cookie cutters.

**2** Cut out the shapes, then use the shapes to cut out the fabric you have chosen to cover your shapes. Cut one for the back and one for the front, remembering that you may need to reverse the design for some of the shapes. Using the white craft (PVA) glue, attach a wooden skewer between two pieces of card.

**3** Glue the fabric to the card shapes. Add any embellishments you like to the decoration—I like to add a touch of glitter to give the bouquet a magical look.

# CHAPTER 4

# winter

MANY SHY AWAY FROM THE ONSLAUGHT OF WET, COLD, OR SNOWY DAYS THAT PEPPER OUR WINTER MONTHS. I GREET THESE DAYS WITH JOY AS I FIND THEM EXHILARATING. I LOVE GETTING UP EARLY, ESPECIALLY ON THESE DARK MORNINGS. THE FIRST CHORE, WHATEVER THE WEATHER, IS TO MAKE SURE THAT THE SWEET CREATURES THAT RESIDE OUTSIDE HAVE FOOD AND WATER TO SUSTAIN THEMSELVES. AS I RETURN TO THE WARMTH OF THE KITCHEN, MY SHAWL STILL WRAPPED TIGHTLY AROUND ME, I PUT ON THE KETTLE. WHILE I WAIT FOR IT TO BOIL I WALK AROUND LIGHTING CANDLES, CHERISHING THE PEACE THAT ONLY CANDLELIGHT CAN BRING. THIS SEASON IS ALL ABOUT THE DELIGHTS OF HOME. THE DECORATING, MUSIC, WRAPPING OF GIFTS AND BAKING FOR FAMILY AND FRIENDS IS BLISS TO ME. THIS JOLLY TIME OF YEAR IS ALSO FILLED WITH JOSTLING THROUGH CROWDS AND JOVIAL PARTIES. THESE ARE ALL TO BE ENJOYED BUT TO SIT QUIETLY AT HOME PRODUCING PRESENTS WITH LOVE FOR THOSE NEAR AND FAR IS A PLEASURE LIKE NO OTHER. WHETHER IT IS A HANDWRITTEN CARD OR SOMETHING MORE ELABORATE, ANYTHING THAT COMES FROM THE HEART WILL BE APPRECIATED. IT IS HOPED THAT THIS CHAPTER WILL INSPIRE YOU TO EMBRACE WINTER INTO YOUR SOUL AND LET THE SPIRIT OF CREATING WARM THE CHILL IN THE AIR.

# rustic stool

I AM ALWAYS ATTRACTED TO SMALL BENCHES AND STOOLS AS THEY ARE A GREAT WAY TO ADD A SPLASH OF COLOR TO A FORGOTTEN CORNER OF A ROOM. EASY TO MOVE AROUND WHEREVER NEEDED, YOU WILL BE TEMPTED TO MAKE QUITE A FEW OF THESE! I HAD THE IDEA FOR THIS STOOL WHEN I BOUGHT A COLLECTION OF OLD BOXES— BY ATTACHING A FEW PIECES OF WOOD, IT SEEMED JUST THE RIGHT THING TO MAKE. ADDING THE LOVELY COLOR OF BARN RED FINISHED IT OFF. I MUST ADMIT I DID GET CARRIED AWAY AND HAVE A FEW OF THESE STORED AS GIFTS.

## MATERIALS

Old box (look for old seed boxes or fruit crates at yard sales and flea markets)

2 pieces of sheet wood for the legs, at least 1½ in. (4 cm) thick

18 nails

1 piece of wood for the support

Red paint (I used water-based eggshell)

## TOOLS

Tape measure

Pencil

Tenon saw

Fret saw

Ruler

Hammer

Paintbrush

**1** Using a tape measure, measure the depth of the inside of the box. Decide how high you want your stool to be and cut two pieces of sheet wood to these measurements.

**2** Using a pencil and ruler, find the center of each leg piece and then draw a "V" shape of any size into each piece, making sure you leave at last 3 in. (7.5 cm) at each side of the "V". This is purely decorative but gives the stool character. Use a fret saw to cut out the "V" shape.

**3** Working on a hard surface, position one of the legs inside the box and hold firmly in place. Use a hammer and nails to secure the box to the legs, using two nails per leg per side. Stand the stool upright and add four nails to each corner to secure the top of the box to the legs. Measure the distance between the two legs and cut the support piece to this length. This extra piece of wood is necessary to support the legs. Slot the support position into position and nail through the legs on each side into the support piece.

**4** Paint the stool, adding two or three coats as needed. Allow to dry fully between coats. Note that this is a decorative stool and is not designed to carry heavy weights.

# quick idea HANGING CRYSTALS

**hint** You could also take some of these crystals and hang them outside on trees before the leaves come out. Then, throughout the year, every now and then you will get a surprise by the tree lighting up as the sun shines. It really, really is magical.

In Scandinavia, light plays such an important role. In the middle of the winter, daylight is scarce and in summer you never feel like heading for bed because it stays light until well after midnight. These crystals, either illuminated by candlelight or positioned to catch the sunlight, capture the beams and send out rainbows of color as well as glistening sparks that create a magical feeling. Old chandelier crystals can often be found at yard sales and flea markets—I feel like I've hit the jackpot when I find a box of them. I'm always reminded of *Pollyanna* by Eleanor H. Porter; if you haven't read it, you must!

## MATERIALS

Old glass crystals from chandeliers (don't be tempted to use plastic crystals as they won't shine as well)

Invisible thread

Branch

## TOOLS

Small pliers

Scissors

**1** Most crystals will have a tiny hole at the top of them, sometimes with a metal clasp attached. These are simple to remove by using small pliers to twist and break the clasp. The metal will then fall out easily.

**2** Thread the invisible thread through the hole in the top of the crystal and pull it through to make a loop. Cut the thread and then tie a knot at the top so you can hang it on the branch. Repeat with as many crystals as you like, varying the length of the thread if you like.

**3** Hang the crystals on the branch and position it where it can catch the light best. Enjoy the light show!

# quick idea RUSTY KEY GIFT TAGS

A while ago I was very fortunate to find an antique tin filled with what seemed like hundreds of old keys. I kept the tin and keys for a long time waiting for the right project. Keys provide many creative possibilities, so I thought they were perfect to use for a present, as a little card, or as a surprise on their own. I made several gift tags and attached keys to them but I also love tying these to a ribbon around a pile of towels in my guest room with some pretty soap to welcome all who stay, or hanging them from a cupboard door. In fact, I think they can go anywhere... for a little bit of whimsical fun!

## MATERIALS

Scrap of linen fabric

Embroidery floss (thread)

Watercolor paper

Ribbon

Old keys

## TOOLS

Needle

Scissors

White craft (PVA) glue

Hole punch

**1** Embroider several small and simple designs on the linen fabric (see pages 107–112). It is best to do this before you cut the linen into small squares, to prevent the fabric fraying too much.

**2** Tear the watercolor paper into small rectangles, approximately 4 x 2½ in. (10 x 6 cm). Cut out small squares of embroidered linen fabric and glue them down onto the pieces of torn watercolor paper.

**3** Using the hole punch, make a hole in a corner of the paper and thread a length of ribbon and key through it. Use them as gift tags—or anywhere you want.

# wooden advent christmas tree

COUNTING DOWN THE DAYS UNTIL CHRISTMAS IS SOMETHING THAT HAS BEEN DONE BY YOUNG AND OLD FOR CENTURIES. THIS WOODEN TREE ADDS A BEAUTIFUL TOUCH TO YOUR HOME AND CAN BECOME A FAMILY TRADITION YEAR ON YEAR. CHILDREN CAN JOIN THE FUN OF MAKING IT BY ADDING THEIR OWN TAGS FOR THE DAYS OF THE MONTH. I USED MINE FOR MANY YEARS IN MY CLASSROOM WHEN I WAS A TEACHER. EACH CHILD WOULD DECORATE THEIR OWN TAG AND AS EACH DAY WAS ADDED A LITTLE CHOCOLATE WAS ENJOYED BY ALL. IT CERTAINLY STARTED THE DAY OFF WITH A SMILE!

## MATERIALS

Pattern paper for template

Sheet of plywood, approximately ½ in. (12 mm) thick

Scraps of giftwrap in coordinating colors

24 nails

24 gift tags

Scraps of fabric and decorative paper

## TOOLS

Template on page 122

Pencil and ruler

Tenon saw

Fret saw

Scissors

Decoupage glue (I use Mod Podge)

Small paintbrush

Hammer

Inkpad and number stamps

**1** Transfer the template on page 122 onto your pattern paper, enlarging as necessary on a photocopier. Use the template to draw the tree shape onto the sheet of plywood then cut out the shape, using a tenon saw to cut the basic shape and a fret saw for the corners. Bear in mind the thicker the wood the more difficult it is to saw out the shape.

**2** Cut squares of giftwrap so that you have a variety of patterns and sizes. Use the decoupage glue to start sticking the giftwrap to the tree, overlapping them in places. Mod Podge gives a lovely finish to the design and will give some protection. Continue until all the tree is covered.

**3** Starting at the top of the tree, attach the nails in the following sequence—you will be creating seven rows of nails:

| | | |
|---|---|---|
| Row 1: 1 | Row 2: 2 | Row 3: 3 |
| Row 4: 4 | Row 5: 4 | Row 6: 5 |
| Row 7: 5 | | |

**4** Decorate the 24 luggage tags using fabric scraps and decorative paper. Use the inkpad to stamp the numbers 1–24 on each tag. You could even write a Christmas message on the back of each one!

# quick idea BELLS AND BUTTONS GARLAND

Decorating for Christmas can be very expensive so it's very satisfying when you can create something sweet and useful just by looking in your sewing drawer. Simply use a few lengths of wire together with little jingle bells and old buttons. This will create a delightful decoration that can be used in so many ways—add them to your tree, drape around a bannister as a garland, tie as a ribbon on a present, or, as I have done here, around a zinc bucket.

## MATERIALS

Gray florist's wire

Jingle bells in a variety of sizes

Old white buttons

## TOOLS

Pliers to cut wire to size

**1** Start by leaving a good few inches of wire without any buttons or bells. Add as many bells and buttons as you like, threading the wire through the holes and twisting or knotting the wire to secure them in place.

**2** The jingle of the bells when you brush past them will delight everyone. I am quite sure that once you start you will enjoy finding places in your home where just one more garland could be added, both inside and out!

# quick idea ANTIQUE QUILT IN OLD WINDOW FRAME

Worn and loved quilts are some of my favorite things. I try and find as many as I can, regardless of the their condition, because I know the amount of work it took to create them and I feel that they should all be treasured as much as possible. This lovely red and white quilt piece was given to me by my Nova Scotian friend Heather. As she presented it to me, she said, "I just know you will do something wonderful with this". The challenge was on. I did not want to cut it up too much, as I love the star pattern. I found just the right window frame complete with glass—look for similar frames at antique fairs or architectural salvage yards.

**MATERIALS**

Old quilt piece

Antique window frame

**TOOLS**

Fabric scissors

Staple gun and staples

**1** Measure the window frame and carefully cut the quilt to fit it, taking into account any piece of the pattern you particularly want to display.

**2** Use a staple gun to attach the fabric to the back of the frame.

hint I also like to write a letter explaining the provenance of both the quilt and the window, put it into a little envelope and attach to the back for someone to find one day.

# old alphabet block christmas tree
REUSING THESE TIMEWORN BLOCKS TO DEPICT A WONDERFUL TIME OF YEAR IS BOTH BEAUTIFUL AND CAPTIVATING; I IMAGINE THIS PICTURE COULD HAVE HUNG IN AN OLD RURAL ONE-ROOM SCHOOLHOUSE YEARS AGO. I AM ALWAYS ON THE LOOKOUT FOR THESE LITTLE BLOCKS AT FAIRS AND FLEA MARKETS. THIS IS AN EASY PROJECT TO DO BUT WILL DELIGHT ALL WHO GAZE UPON IT AS THE USE OF UNIVERSAL WORDS INCLUDES THE WHOLE WORLD IN ITS CHRISTMAS MESSAGE.

## MATERIALS

Flat piece of wood for the backing

Old alphabet blocks

Red paint

Screws

Picture hanging wire

## TOOLS

Tenon saw

Hot glue gun

Paintbrush

Screwdriver

Pliers (optional)

**1** Use a saw to cut the piece of wood to your chosen size—this will depend on the size of your blocks.

**2** Take your alphabet blocks and arrange them into a Christmas tree shape using appropriate words. The most pleasing arrangement is to position them from top to bottom in the following sequence: 1, 3, 4, 4, 5, adding a single block at the bottom for the trunk. Use a hot glue gun to glue them in position.

**3** Using your paintbrush and some red paint, add a heart to the top of the tree (you could also add a star or an angel depending on what you like).

**4** Using a screwdriver attach two screws to the back of the wood then twist the hanging wire around them (use pliers to make this easier if you wish). A surprisingly easy and joyful project that will give maximum impact.

I have collected old zinc buckets for many years. They have so many uses throughout my home and garden and I am always looking for more to add to my collection. I use them as presents filled with flowers, as planters, or simply leave them gathered together on my porch, ready to be used, because they are pleasing to the eye. For a special occasion like a wedding it is always nice for guests to leave a short message for the happy couple—by dotting several buckets around in different places the messages are sure to be delivered.

## MATERIALS

Old zinc buckets

Watercolor paper

Ribbon or short lengths of pretty fabric

## TOOLS

White chalk

Hole punch

Scissors

**1** Use white chalk to add a few hearts to the buckets—draw them freehand to add to the charm.

**2** Tear the watercolor paper into small snippets, just big enough to write a short message on. Punch a hole in the top of each one and thread with a short piece of ribbon.

**3** Leave the buckets where guests will see them, along with a mound of pretty ribboned paper snippets. The kind thoughts, hopes, and wishes will be kept forever and the memory of a special occasion will always be recollected and cherished.

# embroidered recipe envelope

IF YOU ARE ANYTHING LIKE ME, RECIPES RIPPED FROM MAGAZINES AND NEWSPAPERS LIE IN A HAPHAZARD JUMBLE IN YOUR CUPBOARD. I AM ALWAYS SAYING TO MYSELF THAT I WILL ONE DAY GLUE THEM INTO A BOOK BUT THAT DAY NEVER SEEMS TO COME! OPENING MY CUPBOARD ONE DAY THE PIECES OF PAPER FLUTTERED DOWN IN DISARRAY. I DECIDED WITHOUT HESITATION TO CREATE THIS SLIM RECIPE ENVELOPE. IT SLIDES NEATLY BETWEEN RECIPE BOOKS ON A SHELF AND IS EASY TO PULL OUT WHEN HUNTING FOR THAT SPECIAL DISH. IT IS VERY SIMPLE TO QUICKLY PLACE A NEW RECIPE IN THE ENVELOPE, LEAVING A NEAT AND ORGANIZED CUPBOARD IN FRONT OF YOU.

## MATERIALS

Linen fabric

Embroidery floss (thread)

2 sheets of thick white artist's paper, each 10 x 7 in. (25 x 17 cm)

8 in. (20 cm) ribbon

## TOOLS

Fabric pen

Templates on page 121 (optional)

Scissors

Needles and matching sewing thread

Glue stick

Sewing machine

**1** Use a fabric pen to draw your design onto a piece of linen fabric (you can use the template on page 121 or create your own design).

**2** When you are happy with the design, trim the fabric to a square 4 x 4 in. (10 x 10 cm).

**3** Using two strands of embroidery floss (thread), embroider the design). Use a simple backstitch (see page 108) first, then add any details such as little flowers by making French knots (see page 109). The bow on the posy is created using backstitch. Using a different color, weave in and out of the stitches around the bow design to give it depth.

hint This is a lovely idea to make as a wedding present with your favorite recipes written on cards. You could embroider the couple's name in the middle of the wreath with the date of their wedding.

**4** Glue the embroidered fabric square onto one of the sheets of artist's paper. Then, using the sewing machine, carefully stitch the around the fabric edges to secure the fabric to the paper using a small zigzag stitch. It looks best if the thread and fabric are similar colors.

**5** Take both pieces of paper and machine or hand stitch them together using a small straight stitch, leaving the top open.

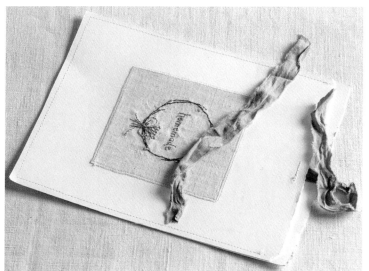

**6** Cut the ribbon in half. Using a needle and thread, stitch the end of each ribbon half to the top inside edge of the paper. Your recipes will now be safe!

# candle box stitchery

WINTERS ARE LONG AND VERY DARK IN SCANDINAVIA. CANDLES PROVIDE MUCH NEEDED RELIEF: LIGHT, WARMTH, AND HYGGE. I HAVE REPRESENTED ALL THE SEASONS IN THIS STITCHERY, AS CANDLES SEEM TO GLOW NO MATTER WHAT TIME OF THE YEAR. I SIMPLY LOVE THIS AND HAVE ADOPTED THIS WAY OF LIFE FULLY IN MY OWN HOME. EARLY SUMMER MORNINGS WILL SEE THE CANDLES GLOWING, TO BE EXTINGUISHED ONCE THE SUN BEGINS TO SPARKLE ON THE DEW. RAINY AUTUMN AFTERNOONS WELCOME FRIENDS AND FAMILY INTO MY HOME WITH A CINNAMON-PUMPKIN SCENTED CANDLE. SPRING IS HERALDED BY THE USE OF A FRESH MINT CANDLE MINGLED WITH THE WARM SCENT OF RAIN. AND FINALLY, WINTER, WHERE CANDLES ARE ONLY BLOWN OUT WHEN IT IS TIME FOR BED. FROM MORNING TILL NIGHT, THE GLOW WARMS THE HEART AND SOUL OF ALL WHO PASS BY. I CANNOT THINK WHEN A CANDLE WOULD NOT BE WELCOME AND, WITH THAT IN MIND, THIS CANDLE BOX FOR ALL SEASONS WAS DESIGNED.

## MATERIALS

Piece of linen, approximately 6 x 6 in. (15 x 15 cm), but you can adapt it to fit the box you are using

Wooden box

Embroidery floss (thread)

Stripwood, ½ in. (1 cm) wide

Cream paint (I use water-based eggshell)

Nails

## TOOLS

Scissors

Template on page 114

Friction pen

Embroidery scissors

Needle

Tenon saw

Paintbrush

Hammer

**1** Cut a piece of linen that will fit across the front of your wooden box. Using the template on page 114 and a friction pen, transfer the design onto the front of the linen.

**2** Using one or two strands of embroidery floss (thread) stitch the design onto the linen. I have used backstitch, satin stitch, lazy daisy stitch, bullion roses, and French knots (see pages 108–112). When you have finished, make sure the threads are tidy at the back and gently press the linen from the back (if you want to iron the front, cover the stitching with a light cloth to protect your work).

**3** Cut four pieces of stripwood to "frame" the stitchery: I used two 6 in. (15 cm) pieces and two 4½ in. (12 cm) pieces. Paint the pieces with cream paint (or to match the color of your box).

**4** Place the finished piece on the box and carefully nail the four pieces of wood to form the frame around the stitchery. I used small black nails for an old-fashioned look.

**MATERIALS**

Selection of pinecones

White paint

Small tin molds

Moss

Glitter

**TOOLS**

Paintbrush

Decorating for Christmas in Scandinavia is all about simplicity. The adage "less is more" is certainly embraced and this allows each decoration to be enjoyed and admired on its own merits. The relaxed, quiet ambiance of a Scandinavian home at Christmas suggests a calm and serene festive occasion. These little glitter pinecone trees add just the right amount of charm to a shelf, a tiny corner in a kitchen, or grouped together to make a delightful table centerpiece. Easy and quick to create, they are also enjoyable to make with children. Just beware, you may end up with a forest of magical trees!

**1** Collect a few pinecones, enough to fit into however many molds you have.

**2** Paint the pinecones using white paint. Add just a few touches here and there rather than covering them completely.

**3** Fill the molds with moss, place the pinecones on top, and have fun sprinkling glitter all over them.

# homemade linen napkin rings

RED, WHITE, AND SILVER ARE COLORS THAT ARE WOVEN INTO EVERY SCANDINAVIAN CHRISTMAS. THE SIMPLICITY OF THIS PALETTE IS BOTH ENCHANTING AND GLORIOUS—ADD A TOUCH OF HOLLY OR IVY AND SOME CANDLELIGHT AND YOUR TABLE WILL BE INFUSED WITH FESTIVE WARMTH. SCANDINAVIANS DELIGHT IN HAVING LARGE GATHERINGS DURING THESE TIMES AND FRIENDS AND FAMILY FREQUENTLY STAY OVER, MAKING IT NECESSARY TO HAVE EXTRA ESSENTIALS FOR ALL. THIS SIMPLE TAKE ON THE NAPKIN RING MAKES SURE EVERYONE HAS THEIR OWN NAPKIN AT THE READY. IN ADDITION, THE SWEET SOUND OF THE JINGLE BELLS AS THEY ARE TOSSED TO EACH PERSON CAN ONLY ADD TO THIS MIRACULOUS TIME OF YEAR.

## MATERIALS

Several pieces of cream or white linen, each measuring 6 x 10 in. (15 x 25 cm)

Jingle bells

Ribbon

## TOOLS

Scissors

Needle and matching sewing thread

Iron

**1** Fold each rectangle of linen fabric in half, long edge to long edge. Backstitch (see page 108) along the short edge and up the long edge, with a ½ in. (1 cm) seam allowance. Trim the seam and then turn inside out through the opening at the top, making sure that the corners are pushed out neatly.

**2** Fold in the raw edges of the fabric at the open end and slipstitch closed (see page 107). Iron the strip of fabric.

**3** Take an 8 in. (20 cm) piece of ribbon and fold it in half. Attach the ribbon at the fold to the end of one length of linen fabric. Using a variety of ribbons helps distinguish whose napkin is whose.

**4** Depending on how thick your napkins are, place your jingle bell where it will hold the napkin together nicely when the ribbon is tied round it. Sew the bell on the strip of linen.

# heart patchwork pillow

OLD QUILTS, FABRIC SCRAPS, EMBROIDERY... WORDS SUCH AS THESE CONJURE UP COZY CREATING TIMES. WHEN I AM DESIGNING A NEW PROJECT, I GATHER TOGETHER ALL OF THESE THINGS AND PONDER, OVER TEA OF COURSE, WHAT CAN BE CREATED. THIS PROJECT GREW FROM THE PURCHASE OF AN OLD QUILT TOP. IT WAS BEAUTIFUL, PIECED BY HAND YET IT HAD NEVER BEEN QUILTED. I ALWAYS HOPE, WHEN TURNING OLD HANDMADE THINGS INTO NEW CREATIONS, THAT THE FORMER QUILTER WOULD BE HAPPY WITH THE RESULTS. I ADDED A FEW HEARTS USING FABRICS TO COMPLEMENT HER OWN. I THINK SHE JUST MIGHT BE SMILING.

## MATERIALS

A selection of prairie print and gingham fabrics

Fusible bonding web

17 in. (42 cm) square piece patchwork fabric (use an old quilt top or some fabric with ready-made squares on it)

Red embroidery floss (thread)

17 in. (42 cm) square of backing fabric

16 in. (40 cm) pillow pad

## TOOLS

Iron

Template on page 122

Pencil

Scissors

Pins

Needle and matching sewing thread

Sewing machine (optional)

**1** Following the manufacturer's instructions, fuse the fusible bonding web to the wrong side of several squares of fabric that you will use for the various hearts. Using the heart template on page 122, draw and cut out several heart shapes from the bonded fabrics.

**2** Lay all your heart shapes onto the patchwork fabric and decide where they look pleasing. Remove the backing by peeling the paper away from the back of the hearts and lay onto the right side of the old quilt piece. Iron the hearts onto the fabric. Using two strands of the red embroidery floss (thread) blanket stitch neatly around each heart (see page 108).

**3** Pin the two cushion pieces right sides together and stitch, either by hand using backstitch (see page 108) or with a sewing machine, with a ½ in. (1 cm) seam allowance. Make sure you leave a gap for turning right side out and inserting the pillow pad.

**4** Turn the pillow cover right side out and insert the pillow pad. Sew the gap shut using a slipstitch (see page 107).

# wooden tag garland

IT IS AMAZING WHAT CAN BE MADE WITH SOMETHING THAT SEEMS DESTINED FOR A BONFIRE. I HAD A BEAUTIFUL PICKET FENCE WINDOW BOX BUT OVER THE YEARS IT STARTED TO DISINTEGRATE IN MY HANDS. AS I HUDDLED ALL THE PIECES TOGETHER, I NOTICED THAT SEVERAL HAD HOLES IN THEM AT THE TOP AS IF THEY WERE MEANT FOR SOMETHING. THE ODD SHAPE LOOKED SWEET AND THE CHIPPED PAINT WAS PERFECT. VERY LITTLE EFFORT WOULD BE NEEDED TO MAKE THIS INTO SOMETHING BEAUTIFUL AND PERHAPS EVEN A FUTURE HEIRLOOM. I SALVAGED FOUR ORIGINAL PIECES AND SOME WOOD FROM THE BASE, WHICH I KNEW I COULD SHAPE TO RESEMBLE THE ORIGINAL PIECES. TO ME THEY LOOKED LIKE LUGGAGE TAGS, WITH THEIR HOLES READY TO BE STRUNG. "PURE AND SIMPLE" IS A FAVORITE ADAGE OF MINE AND THIS TAG GARLAND CERTAINLY FITS THIS CONCEPT.

## MATERIALS

Selection of shaped wooden "tags" with holes in the top

White paint (I used water-based eggshell)

Glass glitter (optional)

Strips of linen fabric

String

Jingle bells

## TOOLS

Paintbrush

Black ink pad and assorted festive stamps

**1** Collect all your wooden "tags" and lightly brush with some white paint to look like snow—don't overload the brush and use swift strokes to barely cover the wood. Allow to dry.

**2** Using a black stamp pad add Christmas stamps to the wooden tags. If you like you can sprinkle a little glass glitter onto the black ink; it will adhere beautifully.

**3** Thread each tag with a strip of old linen fabric and tie in a knot; if the fabric has a frayed edge, so much the better!

**4** Thread a length of string through each linen knot, adding a few jingle bells here and there.

**hint** This garland looks beautiful on a banister along with some ivy. Individually, the tags could be used as part of a special Christmas present with the name stamped onto the wooden tag.

# quick idea SPOOL BOOKMARK

Since creating The Cozy Club many years ago, I have had the pleasure of making so many new and awe-inspiring friends. I am always trying to think of innovative designs that would please these crafters for Christmas—as well as being quick and easy to make. I am always on the lookout for old wooden spools at a fairs or flea markets. I think they look beautiful just as they are but making them into something useful brings a spark of joy.

## MATERIALS

Old wooden spools

Fabric scraps

Ribbon

White craft (PVA) glue

Old linen covered buttons

## TOOLS

Needle and sewing thread

Scissors

**1** Decorate the central part of the spool by glueing fabric scraps or ribbon around it.

**2** Cut a length of ribbon (long enough so that the ribbon hangs out of the book) and attach a linen covered button to one end.

**3** Pull the ribbon through the spool and sew two more buttons to the other end of the ribbon. This makes sure that the ribbon will not pull through the spool by accident.

hint If you are giving these as Christmas gifts it is also nice to add a jingle bell or two to the end of the ribbon instead of a button.

# quick idea LITTLE PINECONE WREATH

Walking in a forest on a crisp fall day carrying a basket filled with the sweetest of little pinecones is such a joyful experience. Knowing that these pinecones will soon be made into presents for Christmas is a comforting thought. These small surprises from nature are pliable enough to be coaxed into a circlet that is perfect for hanging on a doorknob, a tree, or the back of a chair. They will glisten and sparkle beautifully in candlelight if a little glitter is added.

| MATERIALS | TOOLS |
|---|---|
| Small pinecones | Wire cutters |
| Wire | Paintbrush |
| Small grapevine wreath | |
| Paint | |
| Glass glitter (optional) | |
| Ribbon | |

**1** Gather as many small pinecones as you will need for several small wreaths.

**2** Attach lengths of wire around the bottom of each pinecone, leaving a tail of wire to attach each one to the wreath.

**3** Twist the pinecones onto the wreath using the wire; continue all around until the wreath is full.

**4** Paint the pinecones (I used a silvery gray) and sprinkle with a little glass glitter as you like. Add a ribbon to the top of the wreath to hang it.

# snowman chair

I HAVE ALWAYS HAD A PENCHANT FOR OLD WOODEN CHAIRS AND IN SCANDINAVIA THERE IS A TRADITION OF PAINTING HUMBLE PINE FURNITURE TO LOOK LIKE SOMETHING MORE ELEGANT. I SAW THIS LONELY CHAIR AT A RECENT BROCANTE FAIR. IT WAS DESPERATE FOR A NEW OWNER. I GOT OUT MY PAINT AND THIS SAD LITTLE CHAIR BECAME A WARM CHRISTMAS RED. THEN SOME WHITE WAS ADDED AND THE TRANSFORMATION BEGAN SO THAT THIS ONCE TIRED ACHAIR HAS NOW BECOME A SEAT OF HONOR. DON'T FORGET TO REMOVE THE CANDLE BEFORE SITTING DOWN!

## MATERIALS

Old chair

Red, white, green, black, and orange paint (I used water-based eggshell)

## TOOLS

Paintbrushes

Template on page 115

Pencil with eraser top

Toothpick

**hint** Why not make this even more festive by hanging some greenery from the back of the chair, or even adding a touch of glitter.

**1** Give your chair two coats of paint, making sure that you let the paint dry thoroughly between coats. I find that matt paint works best.

**2** Using a small paintbrush and the template on page 115, carefully paint a snowman shape at the edge of the seat with white paint. You could also paint him freehand, don't worry about making him too neat!

**3** Using the top of a pencil with a new eraser on top, dab the pencil in the white paint and dot some snow wherever you like on the chair. I only did into one side like it was falling and the snowman was looking up with joy.

**4** Add the features of the snowman: orange for the carrot nose and green for the scarf. Use a toothpick dipped in black paint for the coal mouth and buttons and a fine paintbrush to paint the arms. Let dry.

# decorative stitches

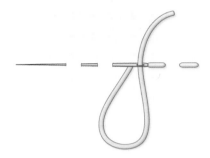

## running stitch

This is a basic stitch that has many applications. It creates a broken or dashed line, and is both functional and decorative. Simply bring the needle up and back down through the fabric, keeping the spaces between the stitches the same size as the stitches themselves.

## slipstitch

Slipstitch is used to close openings—for example, when you've left a gap in a seam in order to turn a piece right side out—and to appliqué one piece of fabric to another. Work from right to left. Slide the needle between the two pieces of fabric, bringing it out on the edge of the top fabric so that the knot in the thread is hidden between the two layers. Pick up one or two threads from the base fabric, then bring the needle up a short distance along, on the edge of the top fabric, and pull through. Repeat to the end.

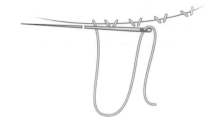

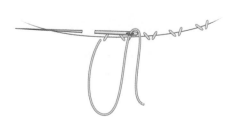

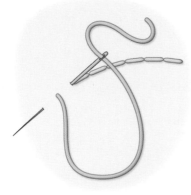

## backstitch

This stitch is both decorative and functional, and it creates a continuous line of stitches, which is perfect for seams and hems. Bring the needle up from the back, one stitch length to the left of your "start" point. Insert it one stitch length to the right and then bring it up again one stitch length in front of the point where the needle first emerged. Always work back into where the last stitch ended; this will give you a nice unbroken line.

## blanket stitch

This stitch is often used in appliqué and for sealing the edges of fabric. Bring the needle through at the edge of the fabric. Push the needle back through the fabric a short distance from the edge and loop the thread under the needle. Pull the thread through to make the first stitch, then make another stitch to the right of this. Continue along the fabric.

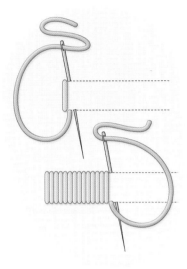

## satin stitch

Satin stitch is a decorative filler stitch. It consists of a series of straight stitches laid close together to completely fill a shape without any gaps.

## french knot

A purely decorative stitch and very versatile, a knot is created on the surface of your work by wrapping the thread around the needle. Bring the needle up from the back of the fabric to the front. Wrap the thread two or three times around the tip of the needle, then reinsert the needle at the point where it first emerged, holding the wrapped threads with the thumbnail of your non-stitching hand, and pull the needle all the way through.

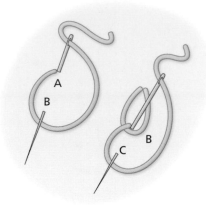

## chain stitch

Bring the needle up at A, then loop the thread and insert the needle at A again. Bring it up at B, looping the thread under the needle tip. Pull the thread through. Insert the needle at B and bring it up at C, again looping the thread under the needle tip. Continue, keeping all the stitches the same length. To anchor the last stitch in the chain, take the needle down just outside the loop, forming a little bar or "tie."

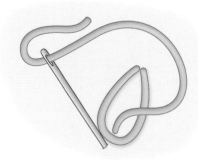

## detached chain stitch and daisy stitch

Work as for a chain stitch (see above), bringing the needle up inside the loop. Take the needle down just outside the loop, forming a little bar or "tie." For daisy stitch, work a group of five or more detached chain stitches in a circle to form a flower shape.

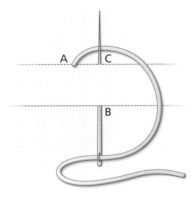

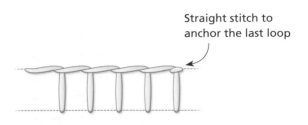

Straight stitch to anchor the last loop

**buttonhole stitch** Buttonhole stitch is similar to blanket stitch but is created in a slightly different way to create a sturdier stitch. It is used around buttonhole edges to prevent the fabric from fraying and is worked from left to right. Bring the needle up through the fabric at point A which lies on the top line. Next, insert the needle back into the fabric at point B which lies at the bottom line slightly to the right from A. The needle must emerge from the fabric at C, which is lying on the top line directly opposite to the B. When you finish the line of buttonhole stitch, make a small straight stitch to anchor the last loop and give a consistent look to the line.

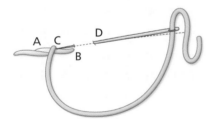

**Stem stitch** Bring the needle up at A, down at B, and, with the thread to the right, back up again at C, halfway between A and B. Take the needle down at D and bring it out at B, at the end of the last stitch.

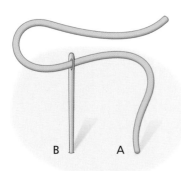 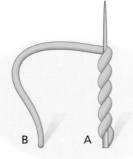 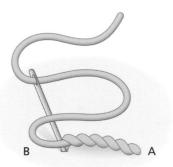

**bullion rose** To make a buillon rose, you need to first know how to make bullion knots. These are similar to French knots, but create longer coils of thread rather than a single knot. Bring the needle up at A and take it down at B, leaving a loose loop of thread—the distance from A to B being the length of knot that you require. Bring the needle back up at A and wrap the thread around the needle five to eight times, depending on how long you want the knot to be. Hold the wrapped thread in place with your other hand and pull the needle all the way through. Insert the needle at B and pull through, easing the coiled stitches neatly into position.

To make the rose, start by embroidering the center of the flower, perhaps with a small cluster of French knots. Bring the needle up near the flower center and form a bullion knot that wraps some of the way around the center. Continue to add more "petals" of bullion knots, overlapping the ends of each stitch slightly. As the flower grows, you will need to create longer bullion knots by wrapping the thread around the needle a few more times and curving them slightly.

# templates

MOST TEMPLATES IN THIS SECTION ARE PRINTED AT 100%. TEMPLATES PRINTED AT LESS THAN 100% WILL NEED TO BE ENLARGED BY THE PERCENTAGE GIVEN. YOU CAN DO THIS USING A PHOTOCOPIER.

## candle box stitchery
page 92

**Stitches**

**Roses**—bullion roses
**Forget-me-nots**—satin stitch
**Snowberries**—French knots
**Rosehips**—satin stitch
**Leaves**—lazy daisy stitch
**Wreath**—backstitch (2 colors)

Roses

Rosehips

Forget-me-nots

Snowberries

## foraging basket
page 72

# boat in a box
page 45

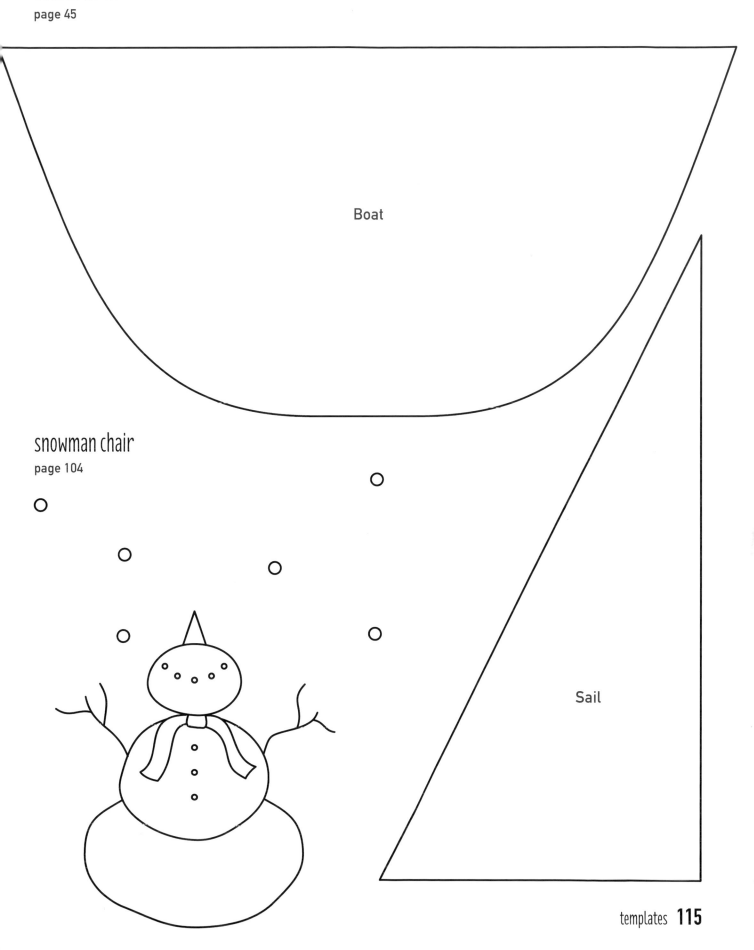

Boat

# snowman chair
page 104

Sail

# driftwood heart

page 32

fold

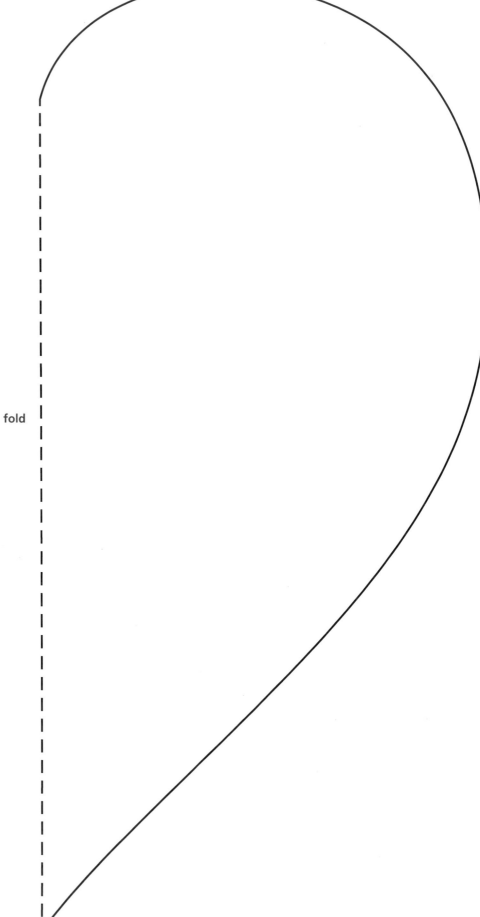

**Stitches**

**Bunny outline and tree**—backstitch

**Eggs**—satin stitch

**Blossom on tree**—French knots

**Leaves on tree**—daisy stitch

**Grass**—straight stitch

**Basket**—satin stitch

**Basket handle**—backstitch

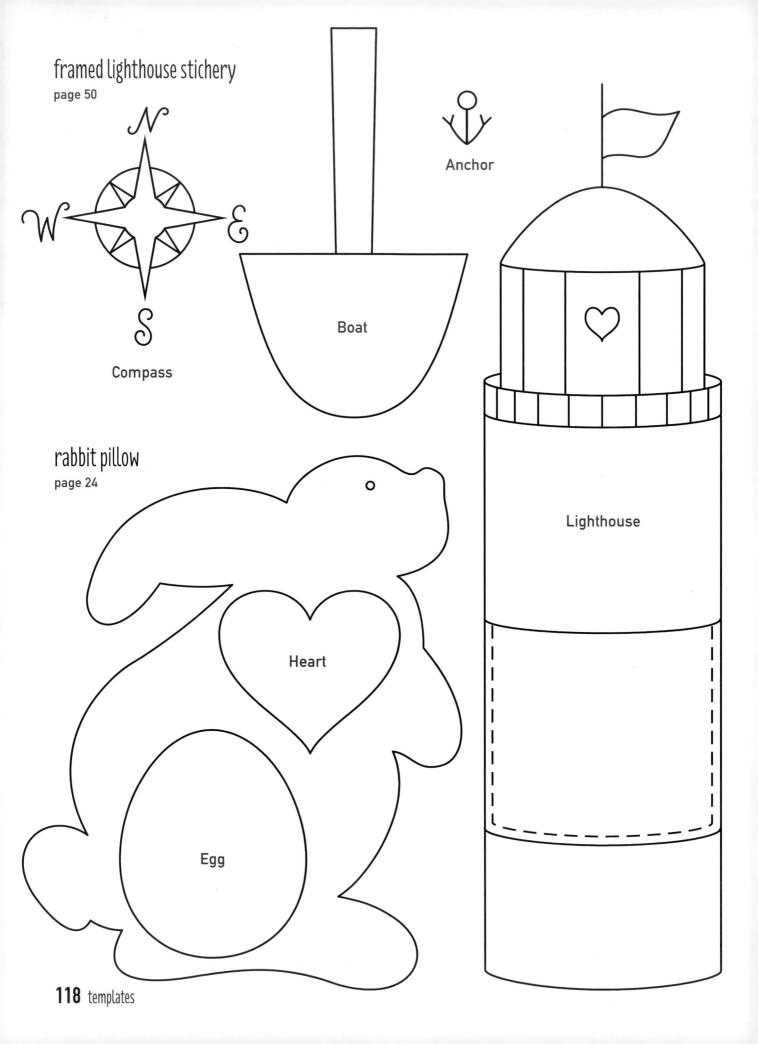

framed lighthouse stichery
page 50

N

W          E

S

Compass

Anchor

Boat

Lighthouse

rabbit pillow
page 24

Heart

Egg

**118** templates

# frieda the friendly witch
**page 66**

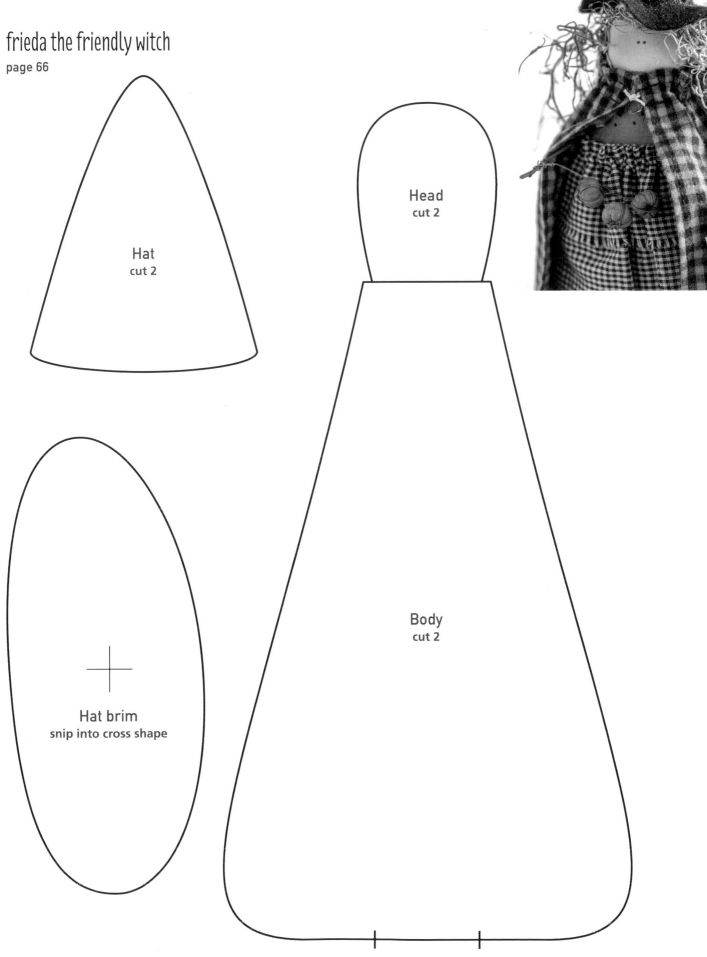

Hat
cut 2

Head
cut 2

Hat brim
snip into cross shape

Body
cut 2

Bat

Cat

Pumpkin

Witch's hat

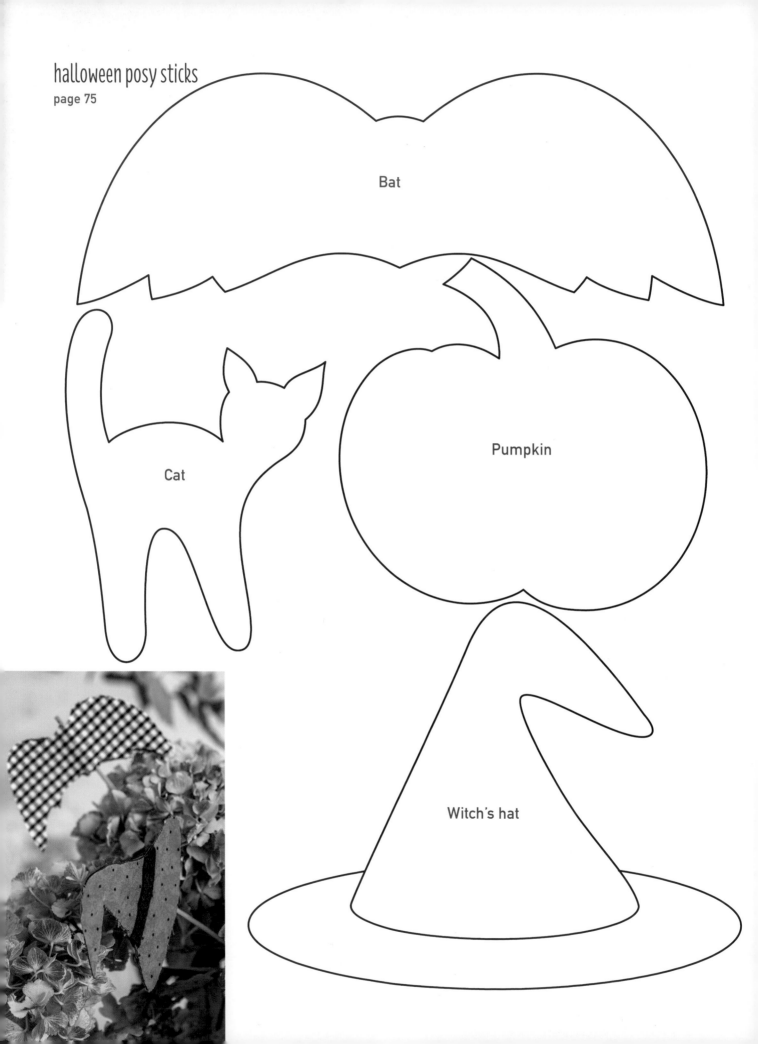

# embroidered recipe envelope

page 89

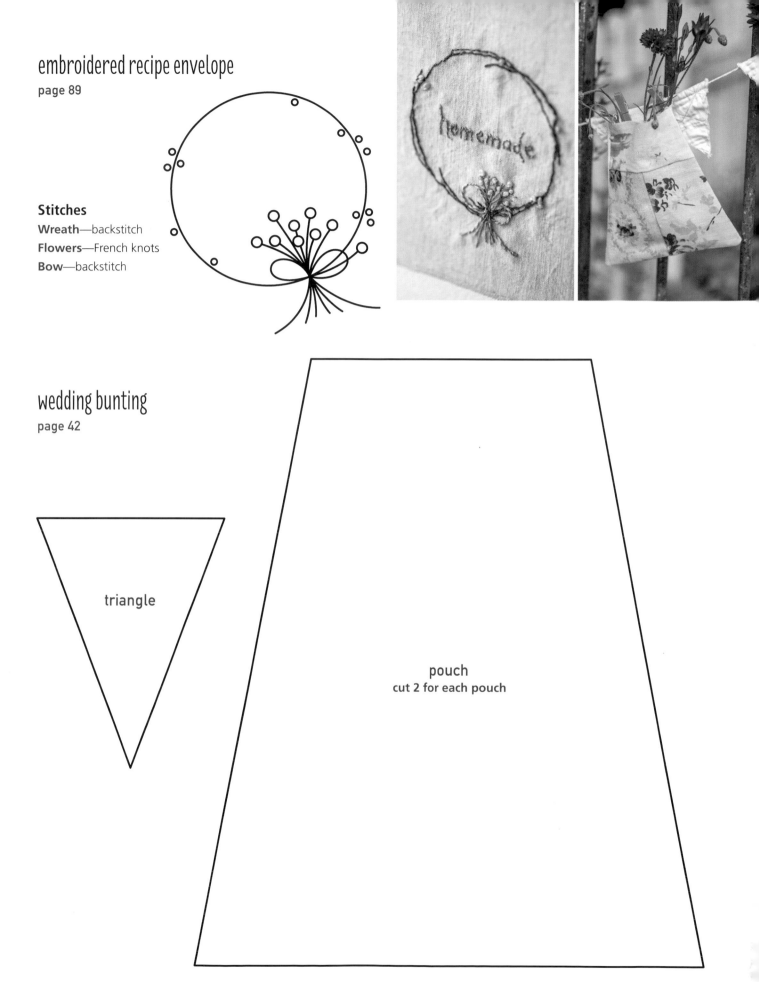

**Stitches**
**Wreath**—backstitch
**Flowers**—French knots
**Bow**—backstitch

# wedding bunting

page 42

triangle

pouch
cut 2 for each pouch

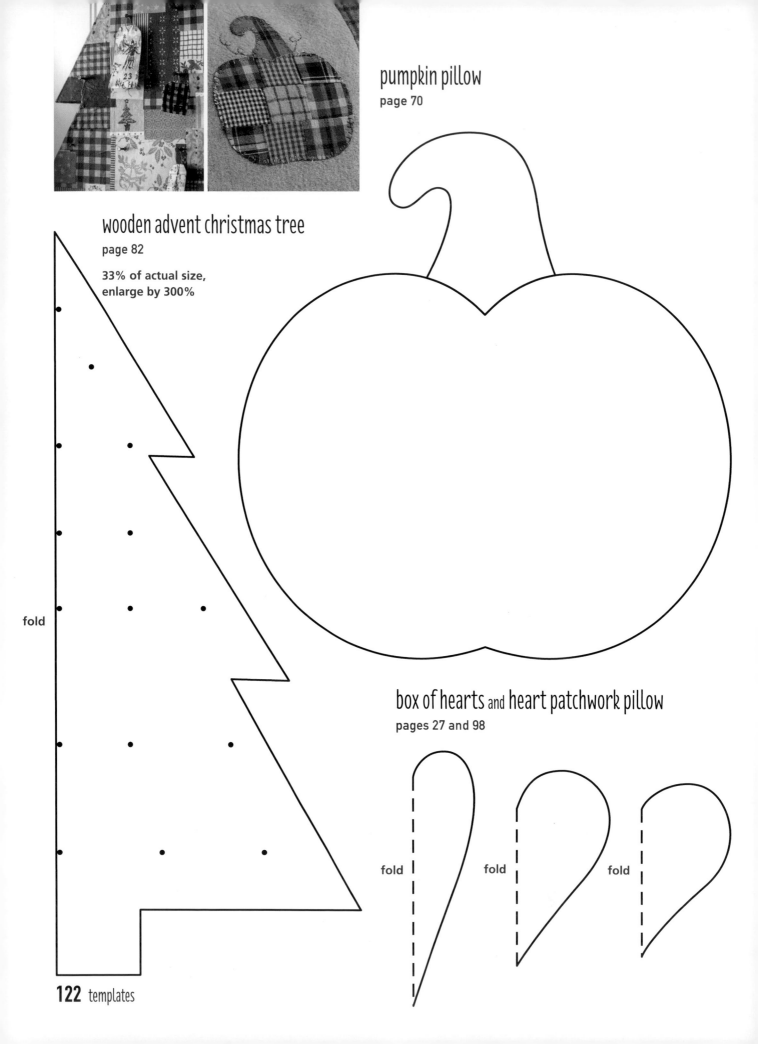

pumpkin pillow
page 70

wooden advent christmas tree
page 82

33% of actual size,
enlarge by 300%

fold

box of hearts and heart patchwork pillow
pages 27 and 98

fold

fold

fold

# spring indoor window box motifs
**page 10**

back stitch

back stitch

French knots

back stitch

back stitch

satin stitch

# Tea light lighthouse

page 34

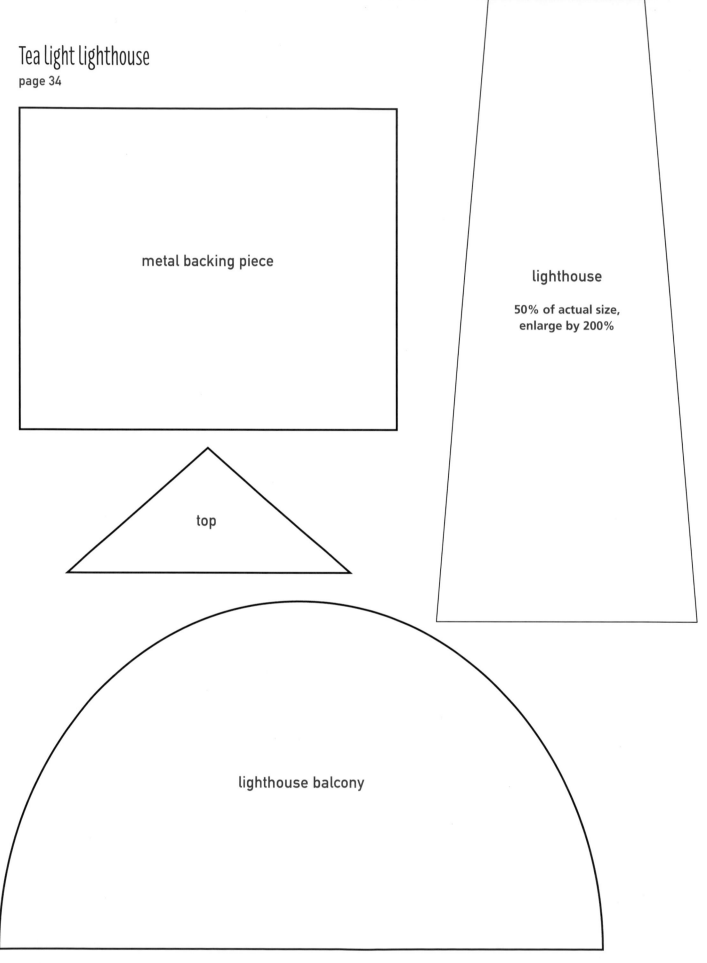

metal backing piece

lighthouse

**50% of actual size,
enlarge by 200%**

top

lighthouse balcony

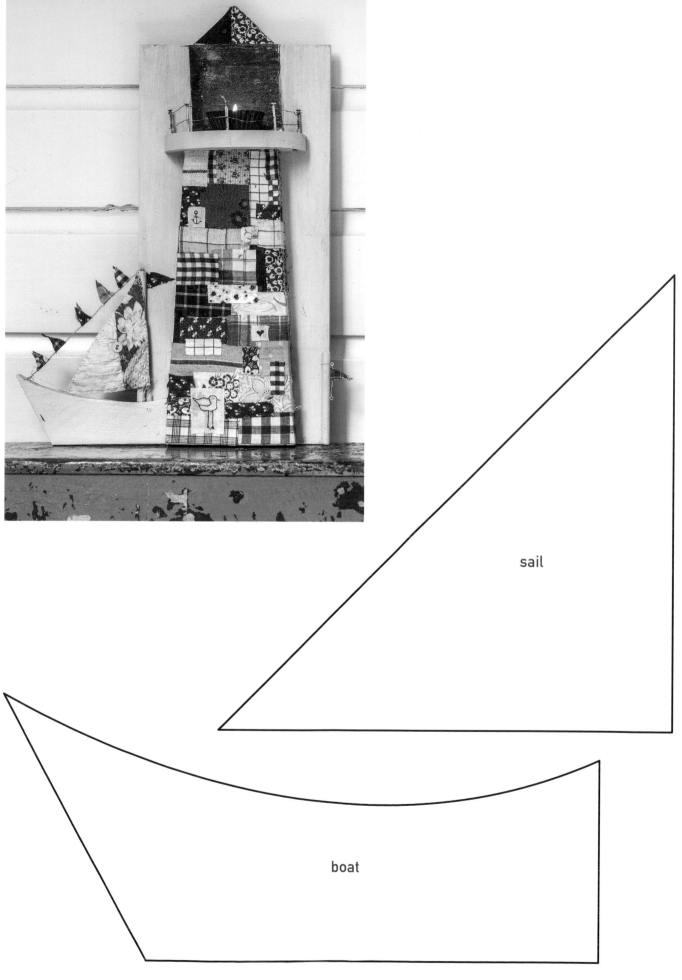

sail

boat

# resources and suppliers

## North America

Going Coastal
41 Queen Street
Chester
Nova Scotia, Canada
www.goingcoastalns.com

Heather Baker
Stell's Cottage
97 Alexandra Avenue
Bridgewater
Nova Scotia, Canada
www.facebook.com/stells.cottage
Instagram: @Stellscottage

www.joann.com

www.michaels.com

MyHome Bay
3 Edgewater Street
Mahone Bay
Nova Scotia, Canada
www.facebook.com/myhomebay
Instagram: @myhomebayns

## UK

Caroline Zoob Designs
www.carolinezoob.co.uk

www.thecountrybrocante.co.uk

www.countryliving.co.uk

www.decorativelivingfair.co.uk

www.hobbycraft.co.uk

www.johnlewis.com

Karen Thomas
Instagram: @ostrichandsilkworm_
brocante

Nutley Antiques
High Street
Nutley, Uckfield
TN22 3NF
Instagram: @nutleyantiques

Penny Menato
www.rosablue.co.uk

Sonia Boriczewski
The Old Haberdashery
33a High Street
Ticehurst
www.theoldhaberdashery.com
Instagram: @theoldhaberdashery

## Europe

www.vintagehouse.dk

Livsstil Pa Egholm Slot
Trehojevej 41
Kirke-Hyllinge
Roskilde, Denmark
@livsstilpaaegholmslot

## Chris's social media

www.thecozyclub.co.uk

Instagram: @thecozyclubx

# index

# acknowledgments

It is always hard not to be repetitive when saying two simple words to so many people. My thank you to all comes from the heart and I hope you know that I am so thrilled and honored to have been able to create another book. My belief is that the world needs a simpler and a more homespun touch, along with all the technological advances. A balance is important and having a sprinkle of the old-fashioned ways, from hand-stitching to wood-working, gives a feeling of calm and joy. With this in mind, I thank Cindy Richards at CICO Books so much for once more offering me the chance to fulfil the dream of passing along ideas for all to introduce a little coziness into their lives.

The invaluable hard work, encouragement, and kindness from Sally Powell, Penny Craig, Yvonne Doolan, Jane Pickett, Clare Sayer, Gurjant Mandair, Stephen Dew, and Alison Fenton has been so appreciated and I thank you all very much.

To my fabulous editor, Anna Galkina, thanks for your understanding and unending help throughout the entire book. Your reassurance, thoughtfulness, and support has been wonderful. You are a treasure.

What is a book without gorgeous photography? I have long admired Caroline Arber's work so to have her as my photographer was amazing. Her desire to get it just right no matter how long it takes makes the end result very special. Thank you, Caroline!

Kerry Lewis, Sophie Martell, and Clare Richardson are all stylists with immense patience and imagination. Thank you for all your efforts in creating the feeling I wanted to convey, you are all wonderful to work with.

Thank you for all the understanding and love shown by my sweet family: Neil, Nicholas, Meaghan, Stefan, and my mother Brigitte. Words cannot actually convey how much I appreciate all your support and reassurance. Neil, your cheerfulness and too-numerous-to-count cups of delicious tea kept me on track. You make my life complete.

Friendship is never to be taken lightly, and I would just like to thank all my amazing kindred spirits who have always believed in my quest for a homemade lifestyle and joined in on many adventures with me. You are all forever in my heart and am honored to call you my friends.

Finally, thank you to all my social media followers and those who come to The Cozy Club. Your enthusiasm and kindness encourage me daily. Your words and constant positivity fuel my desire to share new crafting ideas with you all.